SHEPHERD'S NOTES

Shepherd's Notes Titles Available

SHEPHERD'S NOTES COMMENTARY SERIES

Old Testament

0-80549-028-0	Genesis	0-80549-341-7	Psalms 101-150
0-80549-056-6	Exodus	0-80549-016-7	Proverbs
0-80549-069-8	Leviticus & Numbers	0-80549-059-0	Ecclesiastes, Song of Solomon
0-80549-027-2	Deuteronomy		
0-80549-058-2	Joshua & Judges	0-80549-197-X	Isaiah
0-80549-057-4	Ruth & Esther	0-80549-070-1	Jeremiah-Lamentations
0-80549-063-9	1 & 2 Samuel		
0-80549-007-8	1 & 2 Kings	0-80549-078-7	Ezekiel
0-80549-064-7	1 & 2 Chronicles	0-80549-015-9	Daniel
0-80549-194-5	Ezra, Nehemiah	0-80549-326-3	Hosea-Obadiah
0-80549-006-X	Job	0-80549-334-4	Jonah-Zephaniah
0-80549-339-5	Psalms 1-50	0-80549-065-5	Haggai-Malachi
0-80549-340-9	Psalms 51-100		

New Testament

1-55819-688-9	Matthew	1-55819-689-7	Philippians, Colossians, & Philemon
0-80549-071-X	Mark		
0-80549-004-3	Luke		
1-55819-693-5	John	0-80549-000-0	1 & 2 Thessalonians
1-55819-691-9	Acts	1-55819-692-7	1 & 2 Timothy, Titus
0-80549-005-1	Romans	0-80549-336-0	Hebrews
0-80549-325-5	1 Corinthians	0-80549-018-3	James
0-80549-335-2	2 Corinthians	0-80549-019-1	1 & 2 Peter & Jude
1-55819-690-0	Galatians	0-80549-214-3	1, 2 & 3 John
0-80549-327-1	Ephesians	0-80549-017-5	Revelation

SHEPHERD'S NOTES CHRISTIAN CLASSICS

0-80549-347-6	Mere Christianity-C.S.Lewis	0-80549-394-8	Miracles-C.S.Lewis
0-80549-353-0	The Problem of Pain/ A Grief Observed-C.S.Lewis	0-80549-196-1	Lectures to My Students-Charles Haddon Spurgeon
0-80549-199-6	The Confessions-Augustine	0-80549-220-8	The Writings of Justin Martyr
0-80549-200-3	Calvin's Institutes	0-80549-345-X	The City of God

SHEPHERD'S NOTES-BIBLE SUMMARY SERIES

0-80549-377-8	Old Testament	0-80549-385-9	Life & Letters of Paul
0-80549-378-6	New Testament	0-80549-376-X	Manners & Customs of Bible Times
0-80549-384-0	Life & Teachings of Jesus	0-80549-380-8	Basic Christian Beliefs

SHEPHERD'S NOTES

When you need a guide through the Scriptures

Hosea/ Obadiah

Nashville, Tennessee

Shepherds Notes®—*Hosea, Amos, Joel, Obadiah*
© 1999 Broadman & Holman Publishers, Nashville, Tennessee
All rights reserved
Printed in the United States of America

ISBN 10: 0–8054–9326–3
ISBN 13: 978-0–8054–9326–9

Dewey Decimal Classification: 224.90
Subject Heading: BIBLE. O.T. HOSEA
BIBLE O.T. JOEL
Library of Congress Card Catalog Number: 98–48097

Library of Congress Cataloging-in-Publication Data

Lintzenich, Robert.
     Hosea, Joel, Amos & Obadiah / Robert W. Lintzenich, editor [i.e. author].
       p. cm. — (Shepherd's notes)
     Includes bibliographical references.
     ISBN 0–0854–9326–3 (trade paper.)
     1. Bible. O.T. Hosea—Study and teaching. 2. Bible. O.T. Joel—Study
and teaching. 3. Bible. O.T. Amos—Study and teaching. 4. Bible. O.T. Obadiah—Study and teaching. I. Title. II. Title: Hosea, Joel, Amos, and Obadiah. III. Series.
  BS1560.L555   1998
  224'.907—dc21   98–48097
                                                  CIP

2 3 4 5 6 7 • 10 09 08 07 06
R

CONTENTS

Foreword vii

How to Use This Book viii

The Book of Hosea 1

Hosea 1 4

Hosea 2 7

Hosea 3 10

Hosea 4 11

Hosea 5 13

Hosea 6 15

Hosea 7 17

Hosea 8 20

Hosea 9 21

Hosea 10 24

Hosea 11 25

Hosea 12 27

Hosea 13 29

Hosea 14 31

The Book of Amos 34

Amos 1 37

Amos 2 43

Amos 3 47

Amos 4 50

Amos 5 53

Amos 6 59

Amos 7 62

Amos 8 67

Amos 9 70

The Book of Joel 73

Joel 1 77

Joel 2 80

Joel 3 84

The Book of Obadiah 87

Obadiah 91

Reference Sources Used 100

FOREWORD

Dear Reader:

Shepherd's Notes are designed to give you a quick, step-by-step overview of every book of the Bible. They are not meant to be substitutes for the biblical text; rather, they are study guides intended to help you explore the wisdom of Scripture in personal or group study and to apply that wisdom successfully in your own life.

Shepherd's Notes guide you through the main themes of each book of the Bible and illuminate fascinating details through appropriate commentary and reference notes. Historical and cultural background information brings the Bible into sharper focus.

Six different icons, used throughout the series, call your attention to historical-cultural information, Old Testament and New Testament references, word pictures, unit summaries, and personal application for everyday life.

Whether you are a novice or a veteran at Bible study, I believe you will find *Shepherd's Notes* a resource that will take you to a new level in your mining and applying the riches of Scripture.

In Him,

David R. Shepherd
Editor-in-Chief

HOW TO USE THIS BOOK

DESIGNED FOR THE BUSY USER

Shepherd's Notes for Hosea, Joel, Amos, and Obadiah is an easy-to-use tool for getting a quick handle on these significant Bible books' important features, and for gaining an understanding of their messages. Information available in more difficult-to-use reference works has been incorporated into the *Shepherd's Notes* format. This brings you the benefits of many advanced and expensive works packed into one small volume.

Shepherd's Notes are for laymen, pastors, teachers, small-group leaders and participants, as well as the classroom student. Enrich your personal study or quiet time. Shorten your class or small-group preparation time as you gain valuable insights into the truths of God's Word that you can pass along to your students or group members.

DESIGNED FOR QUICK ACCESS

Bible students with time constraints will especially appreciate the timesaving features built into the *Shepherd's Notes*. All features are intended to aid a quick and concise encounter with the heart of the messages of these four prophets.

Concise Commentary. The books of Hosea, Joel, Amos, and Obadiah are filled with prophecies, oracles, promises, and instruction to believers. Short sections provide quick "snapshots" of the themes of these books, highlighting important points and other information.

Outlined Text. Comprehensive outlines cover the entire texts of the four prophets. This is a valuable feature for following each prophecy's flow, allowing for a quick, easy way to locate a particular passage.

Shepherd's Notes. These summary statements or capsule thoughts appear at the close of every key section of the prophecies. While functioning in part as a quick summary, they also deliver the essence of the message presented in the sections which they cover.

Icons. Various icons in the margin highlight recurring themes of the prophets, aiding in selective searching or tracing of those themes.

Sidebars and Charts. These specially selected features provide additional background information to your study or preparation. Charts offer a quick overview of important subjects. Sidebars include definitions as well as cultural, historical, and biblical insights.

Questions to Guide Your Study. These thought-provoking questions and discussion starters are designed to encourage interaction with the truth and principles of God's Word.

DESIGNED TO WORK FOR YOU

Personal Study. Using the *Shepherd's Notes* with a passage of Scripture can enlighten your study and take it to a new level. At your fingertips is information that would require searching several volumes to find. In addition, many points of application occur throughout the volume, contributing to personal growth.

Teaching. Outlines frame the texts in these soul-searching books, providing a logical presentation of their messages. Capsule thoughts designated as "Shepherd's Notes" provide summary statements for presenting the essence of key points and events. Application icons point out personal application of the messages of the books. Historical Context icons indicate where cultural and historical background information is supplied.

Group Study. *Shepherd's Notes* can be an excellent companion volume to use for gaining a quick but accurate understanding of the messages of the Minor Prophets. Each group member can benefit from having his or her own copy. The *Note's* format accommodates the study of themes throughout these prophetical books. Leaders may use its flexible features to prepare for group sessions or use them during group sessions. Questions to guide your study can spark discussion of these prophets' key points and truths to be discovered in each of the prophets.

LIST OF MARGIN ICONS USED IN HOSEA, AMOS, JOEL, AND OBADIAH

Shepherd's Notes. Placed at the end of each section, a capsule statement provides the reader with the essence of the message of that section.

Historical Context. To indicate background information—historical, biographical, cultural—and provide insight on the understanding or interpretation of a passage.

Old Testament Reference. Used when the writer refers to Old Testament passages or when Old Testament passages illuminate a text.

New Testament Reference. Used when the writer refers to New Testament passages that are either fulfilled prophecy, an antitype of an Old Testament type, or a New Testament text which in some other way illuminates the passages under discussion.

Personal Application. Used when the text provides a personal or universal application of truth.

Word Picture. Indicates that the meaning of a specific word or phrase is illustrated so as to shed light on it.

THE BOOK OF HOSEA

In the canonical arrangement of the books of the Bible, the book of Hosea appears first among the minor prophets. As such, Hosea introduces the central question of the minor prophets—whether the Lord still loved Israel and had a purpose for them beyond His judgment on their sin. Hosea provided the answer by emphasizing God's continued love for His people and the responsibilities that love placed on them.

AUTHOR

Hosea is identified in the title verse (1:1) as a genuine prophet to whom "the word of the LORD" came. That phrase designates the source of his authority and describes his credentials. Not only are Hosea's oracles (Hos. 4–14) the word of the Lord to Israel, but so also are the prophet's narratives dealing with his domestic problems (Hos. 1–3).

Details of Hosea's married life are used in the book to picture God's love for rebellious Israel. Still, we know little about the man Hosea himself. His father's name was Beeri, but that's all we know about him.

Information gleaned from Hosea's book suggests that he was from the Northern Kingdom of Israel. His familiarity with place names, religious practices, and political conditions in Israel indicates that he was a native.

DATE OF WRITING

Placement of Hosea's ministry during the days of kings Uzziah, Jotham, Ahaz, and Hezekiah indicates that Hosea was a contemporary of the prophet Isaiah. The title verse of the book of Isaiah contains the same list of Judean kings. Since

Reading the Prophets

Prophets intended to evoke faith by proclamation, not merely to predict the future. Thus, reading the prophets with a lustful curiosity is inappropriate. Our primary desire must be to know God, not just the facts of the future.

3 children By an unfaithful wife

With the death of Solomon (922 B.C.), the nation of Israel, brought together under David's leadership, divided into the Northern Kingdom, Israel, and the Southern Kingdom, Judah. Israel consisted of ten tribes and Judah of two of the original twelve tribes.

Hosea also prophesied during the reign of Israel's King Jeroboam II (793–753 B.C.), the prophet's work probably started between 760 and 753 B.C.

Hosea frequently envisions the last days of Samaria (Hos. 9:6–7; 10:7; 11:6). Yet at the end of the book Samaria is still alive, though maybe not for long (13:16). Hosea's preaching must have extended through the reigns of Israel's last four kings—Menahem, Pekahiah, Pekah, Hoshea—and ended shortly before the tragic fall of Samaria to the Assyrian King Sargon II in 722 B.C.

AUDIENCE

The Northern Kingdom during Hosea's day was a country that had experienced great affluence, but one that was also witnessing change and decline. Jeroboam II had managed to bring prosperity and territory to the nation. Hosea, though, prophesied during political chaos in Israel following Jeroboam's death. Four of the last six kings to sit on Israel's throne were assassinated. Hosea's audience had lost their stability.

Hosea also ministered during the period of Near Eastern history when Assyria emerged as a new world empire. Assyria's rise to power under the capable leadership of Tiglath-Pileser III (745–727 B.C.) posed a constant threat to Israel's national existence. Hosea rebuked efforts at alliance with either Assyria or Egypt as the means to national security. His message pointed Israel to another deliverer (13:4).

PURPOSE

Hosea's intent was to wake up Israel to their pressing need for national deliverance. But the prophet had a difficult assignment: to convince the people that the oppressor from which they

The Mighty Assyrian Empire

Tiglath-Pileser III made changes in the administration of territories conquered by Assyria. Nations close to the Assyrian homeland were incorporated as provinces. Others were left with native rule, but subject to an Assyrian overseer. Tiglath-Pileser instituted a policy of mass deportations, taking conquered people into exile to live in lands vacated by other conquered exiles. As Assyria grew more powerful, Israel's days of freedom were running out.

must flee was not so much Assyria, but rather Baalism. They must realize that worship of the Lord could not coexist with the worship of the Canaanite god of fertility, Baal.

STRUCTURE AND CONTENT

The two broad divisions of the book of Hosea are Hosea's marriage (Hos. 1–3) and Hosea's oracles or messages (Hos. 4–14). A pattern of judgment followed by hope recurs in each of the first three chapters. A similar pattern is discernible in the oracles, though the pattern is not balanced as neatly or revealed as clearly.

LITERARY STYLE

The first three chapters of the book are an autobiographical account of Hosea's family life which symbolizes God's relationship to Israel. In between the family material are two oracles (Hos. 2), one of judgment and one of hope.

THEOLOGY

At the heart of Hosea's theology was the relationship between God and Israel. The Lord alone was Israel's God. Israel was the Lord's elect people. Hosea presented God as a faithful husband and Israel as an unfaithful wife. Hosea's emphasis is not upon righteousness and justice, as is the case with Amos, but on the knowledge of God and loyal love expected of God's people.

Nothing can quench God's love for His people. Like a marriage partner, God was deeply involved in Israel's lives and was pained by their rebellion and unfaithfulness. Their hope in the future was to return to their God in sincere repentance. Then they would experience God's forgiveness and love which made possible a restored relationship.

Most of the book consists of oracles, communications from God which included prophecies of the future and decisions to be made in the present. The kind of oracles in Hosea are pronouncement oracles that condemn sin and tell what is going to happen. Oracles express God's view of present acts or circumstances.

God's Unending Love

What God desired from His people was an unselfish, loyal, and benevolent concern for the well-being of others. What God received from Israel was love "like the morning mist, like the early dew that disappears" (Hos. 6:4). What God did was to pursue Israel with an undying, reconciling love that would not give up, though Israel had committed adultery with Baal.

THE MEANING OF HOSEA FOR TODAY

Often God's people, in Hosea's day and now, have failed to demonstrate total love for Him. But God stands ready to forgive and restore those who turn to Him in repentance. In buying Gomer's freedom, Hosea pointed ahead to God's love perfectly expressed in Christ, who bought the freedom of His bride, the church, with His own life.

HOSEA 1

- - - -

The first section of the book (Hos. 1–3) introduces Hosea's marriage and family life.

GOD LOVES HIS UNFAITHFUL PEOPLE (1:1–2:1)

The narrative in Hosea 1:2–2:1 and the first-person narrative in 3:1–5 establish the ambivalence in God's relation to Israel. On the one side, Israel's apostasy and violation of covenant agreements merited God's judgment and a "divorce" from God. On the other side, God's determined love for His people would not allow that estrangement to continue.

The Title of the Book (1:1)

The title verse of the book lists four Judean kings during whose reigns Hosea ministered: Uzziah, Jotham, Ahaz, and Hezekiah. Dates for the reigns of these kings would place Hosea's prophetic ministry some time around 740 B.C. (when Uzziah became king), continuing until possibly 715 B.C. (when Hezekiah became king).

Jeroboam II (793–753 B.C.) is the only Israelite king named in the title. Some oracles in the book, however, suggest that Hosea's prophetic work in Israel continued years after Jeroboam's kingship, at least until near the end of the Northern Kingdom (c. 725 B.C.).

Hosea's Wife and Children (1:2–9)

Hosea was given a difficult family assignment. He had to endure a broken heart and a broken marriage along with public indignation and disgrace. God called him to marry an adulterous woman—Gomer, the daughter of Diblaim. Her unfaithfulness to Hosea became a sort of living parable of Israel's unfaithfulness to God.

Gomer bore three children to Hosea, each of which was named to symbolize some aspect of Israel's condition. The first son was named "Jezreel" (1:4) as a symbol of the evil nature of the dynasty of Jehu, which began with much bloodshed in the city of Jezreel (2 Kings 10:6–11).

Hosea's daughter was named "Lo-Ruhamah," meaning "not loved" (1:6). Her name symbolizes that Israel had forfeited God's love by rebelling against God and serving foreign gods. After Israel fell to the Assyrians in 722 B.C., Judah continued to remain independent, even surviving the attack by the Assyrian king Sennacherib in 701 B.C. By saving Judah at that time, God showed His continuing "love to the house of Judah" (1:7).

The youngest child was a boy named "Lo-Ammi," meaning "not my people" (1:9). His name symbolized Israel's lost relationship with God due to their sin and breaking of the covenant.

What Was Gomer's Sin?

Various explanations have been suggested for why Gomer is called an "adulterous wife" (Hos. 1:2). She could have been a common prostitute or perhaps a cultic prostitute engaged in the fertility rituals of Baal. Or she might have been an ordinary woman who became unfaithful after her marriage to Hosea.

The Violent Jehu

Jehu embarked on a violent and bloody course that finally led him to Israel's throne. Along the way, he was responsible for the deaths of Joram, king of Israel; Ahaziah, king of Judah; Jezebel, the still-powerful former queen; and some seventy surviving members of the household of Israel's late King Ahab. At Jezreel, Jehu massacred any person associated with the house of Ahab, including Ahab's friends and priests (Hos. 1:4; 2 Kings 10:10).

To Abraham and the patriarchs, God promised numerous descendants, as "the sand of the sea" (Gen. 32:12). To Moses, God promised that the Israelites would be His people (Exod. 6:7). To David, God promised the throne of a united Israel and Judah (2 Sam. 5:2–5).

Jezreel

The northern city of Jezreel, which guarded the corridor to Beth Shan, was the site of the royal residence of Israel's kings Omri and Ahab. The name *Jezreel* means "God sows," and Hosea's mention of a great "day of Jezreel" (Hos. 1:11) may symbolize God's sowing seeds of prosperity after Israel had faced judgment.

■ *God sometimes calls us to tasks that are diffi-*
■ *cult, demanding, and, in our view, unpleas-*
■ *ant. Can we be obedient in these less enjoyable*
■ *assignments, trusting that the outcome will*
■ *reveal a divine plan that towers above the dif-*
■ *ficulties of our earthly experience?*

God Promises a Future Reversal (1:10–2:1)

The naming of Hosea's children indicated the withdrawal of God's love and forgiveness from His people. Because of the broken covenant, the kingdom of Israel would be terminated and its people sent into exile. God had obtained a divorce from adulterous Israel.

God's love, not willing to give up on a wayward people, would seek for renewal and restoration. God's love would find some way to fulfill the divine promises to Abraham, Moses, and David.

Each of the main sections of the book of Hosea closes with a note of hope. Linked to the announcement of God's judgment is a promise of God's love and of a restoration to take place after judgment. The names "My people" and "My loved one" (2:1) symbolize that a reunited Israel and Judah, as brothers and sisters, will know they are God's people and are loved of God.

- *Hosea used the image of married love to teach*
- *us to understand both the faithlessness of*
- *Israel and the faithfulness of God. The*
- *prophet's own relationship with an adulterous*
- *wife allowed Hosea the insight that God had*
- *not given up on Israel in spite of her faithless-*
- *ness. God desires our steadfast love and He*
- *calls to us, offering restoration and renewal.*

QUESTIONS TO GUIDE YOUR STUDY

1. At what time in history did Hosea prophesy?
2. How does the breaking of a marriage vow by an adulterous marriage partner reflect the same situation as a sinner breaking his or her covenant with God?
3. What were God's promises regarding Judah and Israel?

HOSEA 2

Adultery and Idolatry

GOD SEEKS RECONCILIATION WITH HIS PEOPLE (2:2–23)

Chapter 2 of the book of Hosea is a long speech by the Lord on the themes of Israel's apostasy and God's unfailing love.

God's Legal Actions Call for Reform (2:2–5)

The scene is a court proceeding. God brings charges against His wife (the nation of Israel). The children (individual Israelites) are summoned to testify against their mother, for she has been unfaithful, going after her lovers (Canaanite gods).

Israel, the unfaithful wife, was called on to reform her ways. If she continued to seek lovers,

Several Old Testament prophets, like Jeremiah (Jer. 3:6–10), used adultery as a metaphor to describe unfaithfulness to God. Those who participated in pagan religious practices were unfaithful to the exclusive covenant that God established with His people. To engage in such idolatry was to play the harlot (Hos. 2:5; 4:12).

Better Off Than Now

The adulterous Gomer eventually decided to go back to her first husband, only because she realized that with him she had been "better off" than she was in her current state of adultery (Hos. 2:7). Many people ignore God while their lives are mostly trouble free. Then, when difficulties come, they pray. God wants to hear our prayers of gratitude when life is good, not just when circumstances are bad.

---

then God threatens to "strip her naked" (2:3). Supporting a woman with food and clothing was the legal duty of a husband (Exod. 21:10), but this wife (Israel) had sought her support from lovers (the god Baal).

Turning Back to God (2:6–13)

God made a divorce declaration: "she is not my wife" (2:2), but His true purpose was reconciliation. First, He placed obstacles in her path to turn her back, making her realize she was "better off" with her first husband (2:7).

In addition to placing obstacles in her path, God would take away the fertility of the land. Baal was worshiped as a fertility god who died and returned to life. Baal's resurrection came with the return of the rains, bringing new life to the earth. Israel must return to the Lord, accepting Him as the one God responsible for rain and the produce of the land—grain, wine, vines, and fig trees.

God would also interrupt Israel's empty worship practices. The fertility aspect of the Canaanite gods was an inviting snare to the Israelites. A great deal of syncretism occurred, mixing elements of Baalism with worship of the Lord. Monthly new moon celebrations, annual festivals, and Sabbath observances were done in the name of the Lord, while gold, silver, and jewelry were dedicated to Baal worship.

■ *God's mercy was bound up with His cove-*
■ *nant with Israel. The Law of Moses pre-*
■ *scribed a punishment of death for those*
■ *guilty of adultery (Lev. 20:10). Yet, God in*
■ *His mercy sought not death but renewal for*
■ *His adulterous wife. God's mercy is the*
■ *source of our lives.*

God Initiates a New Covenant (2:14–23)

At some future time, beyond judgment, God would woo Israel to love Him as she had when He delivered her from Egypt. He would take her back to the desert where she had wholly depended on Him during forty years of wilderness wandering. There, in the desert, God would transform the valley of Achor into "a gateway of hope" (NLT). Hosea portrays the day when Israel would no longer worship Baal, but as the faithful bride would again refer to Yahweh, her God, as "my husband" (2:16–17).

Trouble at Achor

The place name *Achor* means "trouble," "affliction" or "taboo." The Valley of Achor was where Achan and his household were stoned to death (Josh. 7:24–26). Centuries later the place became the subject of prophetic promises uttered by Isaiah (Isa. 65:10) and Hosea (Hos. 2:15).

■ *Divorce is what the adulterous wife Israel*
■ *deserved; mercy and renewed covenant*
■ *blessings are what she received. God's ever-*
■ *lasting love is expressed as His mercy in for-*
■ *giving sinners and in rescuing or blessing*
■ *those who do not deserve His attention.*

QUESTIONS TO GUIDE YOUR STUDY

1. What difficulties and changes of fortune facing you now might be opportunities in which God is calling you to return in faithfulness to Him?

Baal the Master

In Hebrew, the term *baal* was a common word for "lord" or "master." The word was also the name of the supreme god of the Canaanites, Baal. Because the word would remind the people too easily of the Canaanite Baal, they should no longer use the word for the Lord. He was their true husband.

2. What steps can you take to renew a personal, intimate relationship with God?

3. Betrothal was an act of engagement in Bible times, but it was binding as marriage is today. How binding is your commitment to God?

HOSEA 3

RECONCILIATION WITH HIS WIFE (3:1–5)

The metaphor of Hosea's family life and God's covenant relationship with Israel continues in chapter 3. Hosea loved his wife, though she was adulterous. This reconciliation is symbolic of God's love for idolatrous Israel. Hosea's marriage story (3:2–3) is the analogy through which we can understand Israel's destruction and restoration (3:4–5).

Hosea Loves Again (3:1–3)

God's command to Hosea was to "show your love to your wife again" (3:1). Such a command would be difficult to obey with a woman who had broken her lifetime commitment to her husband. Only through self-giving love was Hosea able to respond to God's instruction.

A redemption price had to be paid in order for Gomer to regain her freedom. Possibly her practice of prostitution had forced her into slavery. Hosea expressed his love in action as well as feeling, redeeming Gomer by paying the required price of silver and barley.

The common element between Hosea's marriage and Israel's covenant is a high level of unselfish love. Hosea loved Gomer "as the LORD loves the Israelites" (3:1). As Gomer had lost her

Raisin Cakes

Raisin cakes were a food prepared by pressing dried grapes together. Judging from the preaching of the prophets Jeremiah (Jer. 7:18) and Hosea (Hos. 3:1), these cakes must have been used in the worship of pagan deities. In Jeremiah's time, women made cakes in the image of the goddess known as "the Queen of Heaven" (Jer. 44:19).

freedom, so would Israel, no longer able to govern themselves with their own ruler or to maintain their own worship traditions (3:4). But after a period of discipline in exile, the Israelites could return to the Lord, who would again bestow His blessings.

HOSEA 4

The second section of the book of Hosea (Hos. 4–14) consists of a series of judgment oracles, interrupted by two oracles of hope (Hos. 11:1–11; 14:1–8). Most of the oracles in the section concern the dominant theme of the book: God's unrelenting love for His wayward people and Israel's unreliable love for God.

GOD'S CONTROVERSY WITH HIS PEOPLE (4:1–8:14)

Speeches by the Lord rehearse the sins of Israel and the inevitable problems that will follow.

Unfaithful People Break Covenant Commitments (4:1–3)

The proclamation formula "Hear the word of the LORD" introduces God's charge against Israel. His people had broken their covenant with God, so He was taking them to court. They were charged with showing no faithfulness or love to God. Now there was no knowledge of God in the land. The evil consequences of their sin affected every creature in the land, including animal life (4:3).

Unfaithful Priests Bring Judgment (4:4–14)

The function of priests went far beyond sacrificing at the altar and leading worship in the shrine. They were also responsible for blessing the people, determining the will of God, and

Prostitutes in Israel

The wisdom literature of the Old Testament shows the way for a person to live in harmony with God's order for creation. Thus, the book of Proverbs provides strong counsel against prostitution, warning a young man that "a prostitute is a deep pit" (Prov. 23:27; see also Hos. 3:3). Love that does not cost the lover anything is not worthy of being called "love." Both Hosea and God paid a high price to love. An emotional price is paid whenever a loved one goes after other lovers. A physical price is paid whenever a loved one must be redeemed from a broken life. Hosea and God paid the whole price with real love.

The prophet Amos faced similar opposition from Amaziah, priest of Bethel (Amos 7:10–11).

The Double Standard

Prostitutes had an ambiguous status in Israelite society. They were tolerated as long as they were not married, but their profession was not socially acceptable. Hosea criticized the attitude which called for the punishment of prostitutes, while tolerating the men with whom these acts were committed (Hos. 4:14). This was a double standard.

Beth Aven

The place name *Beth Aven* means "house of wickedness." Hosea used the name as a description of Bethel. Instead of a house of God, Bethel had become a house of idolatry. Thus, the prophet commanded worshipers to refuse to go there (Hos. 4:15).

instructing the people in the law of God. The Lord charged the priests with failing to carry out their proper functions.

A second charge against the priests was their involvement in cult prostitution. In the Canaanite fertility cults (including Baal worship), sacred sexual intercourse by priests and cult prostitutes was an act of "worship" intended to emulate the gods and share in their powers of procreation. The goal was to compel the gods to preserve the earth's fertility.

These abuses would bring God's punishment—on people and priests. God would take away the sacrificial system that fed the priests so well. He would hold them—not their daughters—accountable for the cult prostitution that males supported and allowed to flourish.

- *God's people had come to ruin because they*
- *followed the direction of corrupt religious*
- *leaders.*

Judah Warned About Sister Israel (4:15–19)
From Hosea's time on, the name "Ephraim" (4:17) was used as a designation for the Northern Kingdom of Israel. God warned the Southern Kingdom of Judah not to become involved in the idolatry of their sister kingdom, Ephraim. He commanded Judah's worshipers not to visit Ephraim's cultic sites at Gilgal and Bethel (Beth Aven). As far as Ephraim, the "whirlwind" of Assyria's army would take them away in 722 B.C.

QUESTIONS TO GUIDE YOUR STUDY

1. Israel's priests had allowed the "business" of sacrifice to overshadow the spiritual nature of the offerings, so God rejected them as priests. What "business" aspects of your church life might hinder your spiritual worship if they are allowed to predominate?

2. Sex is such a strong force in the human psyche that it can be instrumental in leading a person away from sincere worship of God. What has the modern church substituted for the "cult prostitution" of ancient worshipers?

3. The male priests could not blame the female harlots and cult prostitutes for what went on in the shrines. Why is it easier to blame someone else than to admit our personal responsibility and repent?

HOSEA 5

Chapter 5 reflects two of Israel's major problems. Their religious problem of chasing after the Canaanite fertility cults is condemned in the oracles of 5:1–7. Another problem that Israel as well as Judah faced was political: they had turned to Assyria and Egypt for help instead of to God (5:8–6:6).

God Condemns Israel's Leaders (5:1–7)

The proclamation formula "hear this" (5:1) issues a judgment against three areas of leadership. "Priests" represented the religious leadership. The "royal house" included the king and his court. "Israelites" could refer specifically to the elders, who represented the various clans

The Name of Ephraim

The name "Ephraim" was originally given to the younger son of the patriarch Joseph (Gen. 41:52). This son was the progenitor of the tribe of Ephraim, which occupied a region northwest of the Dead Sea. Ephraim played an important role in Israelite history as the leading tribe of the Northern Kingdom, and eventually the name was used to designate the entire nation of Israel (Hos. 5:3).

Moving the Boundary Stone

Many ancient peoples used a pillar or heap of stones to serve as a boundary marker. Babylonians, Egyptians, Greeks, and Romans had law codes prohibiting the removal of such a landmark, since to do so often cheated a poor landowner. So Proverbs warns, "Do not move an ancient boundary stone or encroach on the fields of the fatherless" (Prov. 23:10).

and tribes. A hunt describes figuratively how these groups had misled the people; these unfaithful leaders were portrayed as hunting the people with snares and nets.

- *Sin creates a barrier between God and*
- *human beings. The person who constantly*
- *and consistently follows a sinful course will*
- *become so enmeshed in sin that he or she will*
- *be enslaved to sin.*

Inescapable Judgment upon the Sister Nations (5:8–6:6)

The judgment oracles in 4:1–5:7 fit with the last years of Jeroboam's reign (793–753 B.C.), reflecting the prosperity of the nation at that time. The wealth the people enjoyed allowed them to pursue a self-indulgent lifestyle that left little need to seek the Lord. The oracles of 5:8–6:6 reflect a later period of unrest, the Syro-Ephraimite crisis, when King Rezin of Syria and King Pekah of Israel (Ephraim) joined forces to attack Judah (735–733 B.C.).

Judah was not any better than Israel at that time. Ahaz, who became Judah's king in 735 B.C., participated in idolatrous practices (2 Kings 16:1–4). Hosea condemned the ruthlessness of unnamed rulers of Judah, comparing them to people who "move boundary stones" (5:10). Moving a boundary stone meant changing the traditional land allotments, which was considered theft.

- *While Israel and Judah suffered at the hands*
- *of Assyria, the Lord God was absent. When*
- *we desert God, He withdraws, waiting until*
- *we seek Him again with sincere repentance*
- *(5:15).*

QUESTIONS TO GUIDE YOUR STUDY

1. Who are the religious leaders that you have chosen to follow? How do you evaluate them in terms of their knowledge of God and their obedience to Him?
2. What are the signs of genuine repentance?
3. What characteristic of God makes Him withdraw from us until we show signs of repentance?

Winter and Spring Rains

Palestine was a land dependent upon the yearly rains to ensure an abundant harvest and an ample food supply for the coming year. Two seasons of rain were crucial: the early winter rains during October and November and the later spring rains in February and March (Hos. 6:3). One of Israel's theological struggles in attempting to blend Canaanite and Hebrew religion concerned the rain. Since the presence or absence of rain symbolized the deity's blessing or displeasure, Hosea wanted the people to know which deity—the Lord or Baal—really had the power to withhold or to send rains.

HOSEA 6

A Choral Response (6:1–3)

Israel had broken their covenant with the Lord by going after Baal, the fertility god of Canaanite religion. As a result, the Lord withdrew to His place (5:15), which possibly refers to Mount Zion (Amos 1:2). There He would wait until Israel would seek Him "earnestly" and "admit their guilt."

A liturgical song (6:1–3) reveals a penitent people, but the sincerity of their repentance is questionable. Surface repentance does not satisfy the sovereign God, who wants more from His people than mere regret of past actions.

Israel's song of penitence was disappointing. They vowed to "acknowledge the LORD" (6:3), but they tried to make Him into a nature god, like the god Baal they had followed.

■ *Presumptuously, the Israelites counted on*
■ *God's reliability, assuming He would return*
■ *to them as surely as the predictable sunrise.*
■ *Our concept of God is erroneous if we think*
■ *He will act according to our expectations.*

God Answers with His Requirements (6:4–6)

God's reaction to Israel's attempt at repentance shows His disappointment. They had compared Him to nature, so He would compare them to "morning mist" and "early dew" (6:4). Their covenantal relationship was as temporary as these natural phenomena.

What God really wanted from Israel was covenantal faithfulness. One aspect of this faithfulness was mercy; to meet God's requirement, they must show mercy to others (Hos. 6:6). If they were truly to acknowledge God, they must do so in their human relationships.

Caring mercy was to affect all levels of human relationships in Hebrew society: husband and wife, father and son, host and guest, king and subjects. It expressed itself in action on another person's behalf and was always reciprocal.

Covenant-Breaking Hinders Restoration (6:7–7:2)

The covenant relationship became so characteristic for Israel and their God that the psalmists in worship called Israel to covenant keeping (Ps. 25:10). Israel, however, was prone to covenant breaking (6:7). From Gilgal to Shechem, the land was strewn with wickedness in which even

Mercy, Kindness, Love

The word *mercy* (Hos. 6:6) translates a Hebrew word extremely rich in meaning. English translations have attempted to capture the meaning of the Hebrew word by "kindness," "steadfast love," "lovingkindness," "loyalty," and "faithfulness," as well as several other English expressions. Each translation pictures a "caring mercy" that seeks to meet the needs of others.

the priests were involved (6:9): murder, prostitution, deceit, robbery.

Keeping the Covenant

"All the ways of the LORD are loving and faithful for those who keep the demands of his covenant" (Ps. 25:10).

- ■ *The people did not realize how deep their*
- ■ *sins had become. They thought that in two*
- ■ *days, maybe three, their difficulties would be*
- ■ *solved. The best solution to our unfaithful-*
- ■ *ness is to understand that sin in any form is*
- ■ *the most serious of humanity's problems.*

QUESTIONS TO GUIDE YOUR STUDY

1. Describe the shallow form of repentance that is popular in some Christian circles today. What is God looking for in an individual that qualifies as genuine repentance?

2. What actions can you take to ensure that the loyalty to God that you declare today will not evaporate in the face of tomorrow's problems? How deep is your loyalty?

3. Why should we continually remind ourselves that our sinful deeds are always before God? Does it matter when temptations surround us?

Hosea and Judah

Hosea, who most likely was from the Northern Kingdom, prophesied primarily to Israel. So we may wonder why often in the book the prophet speaks of or to Judah (Hos. 6:11). While Israel and Judah were two separate kingdoms, the prophets viewed them as one people of God. Just as Amos, a prophet from Tekoa in Judah, could minister to Israel (Amos 1:1), so could Hosea, a prophet of Israel, deliver God's word to Judah, while prophesying mainly to the Northern Kingdom.

HOSEA 7

Hosea condemned Israel for relying on their own strength rather than on God. When they should have sought divine power (7:10), the people turned arrogantly to political power, either through their chosen ruler (7:3–7) or through political alliances with other nations (7:8–16).

Our Sins Before God

Hosea preached a truth about sin that should wake up each of us: our sins are always before God, who remembers our evil deeds (Hos. 7:2). Though sinful acts may be directed against another person, ultimately every sin is against God. Let us confess with the psalmist, "Against you, you only, have I sinned" (Ps. 51:4) and turn in repentance to the all-knowing Creator of all things.

Israel's Kings Fall (7:3–7)

Jeroboam II was a powerful king of the Jehu dynasty who enjoyed a long, peaceful reign. But the period following his death in 753 B.C. was filled with political turmoil. Of the last six kings in Israel, four were assassinated, as political factions fought for control. Shallum and Menahem each led extremist parties which sought the throne by violence.

Such political unrest is reflected in Hosea's later oracles (8:4; 9:15). Wickedness, lies, and intrigue were characteristic of the reigns of Israel's last kings. The hot fire of an ancient cooking oven best depicts the passions, power struggles, and instability of a people who "devour their rulers" (7:7). On the day of coronation, the new king "joins hands" (7:5) with the princes who mocked and ousted the previous ruler.

- *Israel's people confessed God as their ultimate*
- *King (Judg. 8:23). The earthly king must*
- *remember that, as the Lord's anointed leader,*
- *his own authority was derived from God. To*
- *forget that was to reject God's sovereignty.*

Despite the desperateness of their political situation, Israel did not turn back to the Lord, calling on Him for help. None of the kings who ascended Israel's throne tried to rule by relying upon the Lord. Indeed, the assessment "he did evil in the eyes of the LORD" (2 Kings 15:18) is reported for each king from Zechariah to Hoshea (except one, Shallum, who reigned only one month).

Israel's Alliances Fail (7:8–16)

Ousting one king for another did not improve Israel's declining national health, and neither did the numerous associations they formed with other nations. It is possible that Menahem obtained the throne of Israel with Assyria's help. He was little more than a puppet of the Assyrians during his reign. Trusting in other nations eventually led to Israel's fall. The Egyptian King So encouraged King Hoshea to withhold tribute from Assyria, a move that triggered Assyria's three-year siege of Samaria (725–722 B.C.).

Using several images, the prophet Hosea proclaimed the folly of foreign alliances. Israel "mixes with the nations" like cooking oil with flour, but would be seared like a "cake not turned" during cooking (7:8). They did not realize that they were aging and losing strength by trusting in foreigners. Like a senseless dove, Israel was deceived by Egypt and Assyria.

Wail for Baal

Rather than seek the Lord, a rebellious people were wailing on their beds (Hos. 7:14). The scene resembles the wild rituals associated with Baal, such as worshipers who shouted to the Canaanite god while cutting their own flesh (1 Kings 18:28). The Law of Moses specifically prohibited ritualistic cutting. (Deut 14:1).

■ *By turning away from the almighty God,*
■ *Israel resembled a "faulty bow" that could*
■ *not shoot arrows straight to a target (7:16).*
■ *As Christians, we need God's guidance in*
■ *order to hit the target of spiritual growth.*
■ *Whatever our spiritual goals may be, we will*
■ *miss them by relying on alternative religious*
■ *sources.*

QUESTIONS TO GUIDE YOUR STUDY

1. When we associate with unbelievers, what are ways we can influence them to seek the Lord? How might "alliances" with unbelievers influence us to move away from our Christian faith?

2. Belonging to organizations, associations, and coalitions is an effective way to influence the world around us. How might these group relationships compete with or disrupt our personal relationship with God?

3. Israel's arrogance led the people to place confidence in their ability to manage

Making a God

Hosea (Hos. 8:6) and Isaiah (Isa. 44:9–20) considered it ridiculous that someone should worship something made by a craftsman. An idol is made by the craftsman but is powerless to sustain the craftsman or enable him to complete his task. What results is a worshiper bowing not to a God but to a block of wood!

their own affairs. Why is such arrogance a form of rebellion against God?

HOSEA 8

The Unfaithful Reject God's Goodness for Idolatry (8:1–6)

The approaching judgment of God is symbolized by the trumpet blast and circling eagle. Israel's claim of acknowledging God was empty, for they were actually covenant breakers. The sin of the calf idol of Samaria was not worshiping the wrong god, but worshiping the true God in the wrong way. God would not allow Himself to be represented by images made by a craftsman.

The Unfaithful Reap Foreign Domination (8:7–10)

Despite the preaching of Amos and Hosea, Israel could not understand that the direction they were pursuing would lead them into exile. They could not imagine that the foreigners they allied with would one day swallow them, and they would become a "worthless thing" (8:8), oppressed by a foreign king.

The Unfaithful Reap Religious and Moral Corruption (8:11–14)

Hosea condemned the people's faulty concept of sacrifice. Sacrifices were offered at altars with the feeling that God was present there and accepted the offering. But God was not pleased with Israel's many altars, for they had become "altars for sinning" (8:11). The people tended to ignore God's laws, thinking the act of sacrifice ensured spiritual well-being. It did not because by misusing the sacrificial system they had forgotten their Maker.

■ *When we do foolish things, we face the*
■ *destructive consequences of our actions. If*
■ *we sow foolishly to the wind, we will reap a*
■ *whirlwind of destruction (8:7). Israel was*
■ *foolish in how they attempted to worship*
■ *their God while courting favor with*
■ *foreigners.*

QUESTIONS TO GUIDE YOUR STUDY

1. List the various forms of worship and ritual which we follow instead of sacrificing at altars. Do we involve ourselves in some of them merely to gain God's favor? Is He really pleased?
2. Do God's laws seem "alien," as if they could apply to other people, but have no relation to our own lives? If so, look for hidden areas of your life for which these laws offer some application.
3. What would be the consequences of Israel's political alliances?

HOSEA 9 · · · · ·

GOD'S JUDGMENT AGAINST HIS PEOPLE (9:1–13:16)

Israel refused to take covenant commitment seriously. Covenant with the Lord involved Israel's pledge to make no other covenants or treaties (Exod. 34:12, 15). That pledge had been broken by numerous alliances with foreigners. Covenant also involved Israel's obedi-

Appointed Feasts

At three appointed times during the year, all Jewish males were required to appear at the sanctuary (Exod. 34:23). Passover and the Feast of Unleavened Bread was the first festival, occurring in the spring. The second was the Feast of Weeks (also called the Feast of Harvest), celebrated seven weeks later. The third was the Feast of Tabernacles (also called the Feast of Ingathering), celebrated in the fall at the closing of the grape harvest. In exile, the males would miss their "appointed feasts" (Hos. 9:5).

ence to God's commandments as His expectations for His covenant people (Exod. 34:27–28). Instead of obeying the commandments, Israel "regarded them as something alien" (Hos. 8:12). God must declare judgment against His unfaithful people.

The Unfaithful Reap Exile in a Foreign Land (9:1–6)

The Feast of Tabernacles was a time of celebration. It was observed with the ingathering of produce from the threshing floor and the winepress. This was to be a joyful reminder to Israel of God's blessings in the harvest (Deut. 16:13–15). Hosea, though, interrupted the celebration, crying, "Do not rejoice" (9:1).

Produce was the essence of the feast. In the future, however, Israel would not enjoy grain and wine in "the LORD's land"; instead, in exile they would eat the "unclean food" of a foreign land (9:3). Not only would the feasting cease, so also would their sacrificial system of worship. Once in exile, Israel would no longer be able to come to the Temple with their wine offerings and sacrifices.

- *What would Israel do when the appointed*
- *day for their festival arrived, and they were*
- *exiled in Assyria? How sad it is for God's*
  people to take His blessings for granted.

The Unfaithful Reap Punishment (9:7–9)

Hosea's preaching was not popular in Israel, and the prophet faced persecution, as had his contemporary Amos (Amos 7:10–13). The people called the prophet a fool and a maniac (Hos. 7:7). Prophetic activity was sometimes accompanied by ecstatic, irrational behavior, leading prophets to be identified as madmen (Jer. 29:26).

The prophet offered a different perception, seeing himself as a watchman warning the nation of God's approaching judgment. He must warn them that their corruption was as evil as the bloody civil war in Gibeah between the tribe of Benjamin and the other Israelite tribes (Judg. 19–21). Punishment was at hand!

Without God's Love, His People Perish (9:10–17)

Hosea returned to the story of Israel's beginnings in colorful metaphoric language. The Israel of the prophet's time is contrasted with the Israel of Moses' time. Israel's beginnings were pure, but their contacts with Canaanites had brought apostasy.

Before Canaan, Israel was as pleasing to God as "grapes in the desert" and the "early fruit on the fig tree" (9:10). After Canaan, they were as displeasing as the vile Baals that they worshiped. Since they sought Baal to provide fertility, their punishment would be infertility (9:14, 16).

■ *Various places in Israel's past carried a dark*
■ *history: corruption at Gibeah, shame at Baal*
■ *Peor, wickedness at Gilgal. We must remem-*
■ *ber that a life of sin leaves a trail that cannot*
■ *be covered. Eventually, the trail tells the*
    whole story.

QUESTIONS TO GUIDE YOUR STUDY

1. Israel tried to find help from Assyria. When that failed, they turned to Egypt.

Maniac Prophets

In the Old Testament, ecstasy was associated with bands or schools of prophets (1 Sam. 10:5–6; 19:20, 23–24). The ecstatic state was often accompanied with music and rhythmic dance, though the prophetic frenzy was brought on by the Spirit of God. These prophetic expressions led onlookers to characterize prophets as "madmen" or "maniacs" (Hos. 9:7).

Worshiping Baal Peor

Baal Peor (Hos. 9:10) was a Moabite deity that the Israelites worshiped when they had illicit sexual relationships with Moabite women. The guilty Israelites were punished severely for this transgression, and the incident became a paradigm of sin and divine judgment for later generations (Num. 25:1–5; Ps. 106:28).

Pursuing Money or God

Materialism creeps into our society in various forms: the pursuit of wealth as an end in itself; the desire for luxury; personal indulgences. Somehow we justify spending lavishly on ourselves. Hosea's Israel enjoyed their prosperity in this manner (Hos. 10:1). As Christians, we must learn to possess money and not be possessed by it. Channel your wealth toward serving people and spreading the gospel.

Are there times when you have tried several different remedies before discovering that God's solution was best?

2. Israel labeled Hosea as a madman who should not be taken seriously. How do you dismiss advice from others that conflicts with your personal viewpoints?

3. What were the factors that changed God's delight with Israel in the desert to His hate for them at Gilgal?

HOSEA 10

Deceitful People Make for Bad Times (10:1–8)

God gives physical resources to humans to control and enjoy, but the human tendency is to lift these resources to replace God as the center of life. In Canaan, Israel became a prosperous nation, symbolized agriculturally as "a spreading vine" (10:1). One sign of prosperity was a buildup of religious activity and the multiplying of altars and sacred sites. But the ornate altars could not hide the people's deceitful hearts.

Planting Wickedness Reaps Evil (10:9–15)

With agricultural imagery Hosea pictured God's judgment on Israel. The people of Ephraim who had planted wickedness and deception would reap judgment and punishment. Like a young heifer, they would be yoked and forced to plow. Only if they sowed righteousness could they reap God's unfailing love.

Since Israel had trusted in their "many warriors" (10:13), Hosea's imagery changed from agriculture to the military, describing the coming devastation. The mysterious figure of "Shalman"

(10:14) could be an abbreviation for Shalmaneser V of Assyria who led the siege on Israel in 725 B.C. Shalman's name was synonymous with violence and ruthlessness. The infamous battle at Beth Arbel is unknown to us, but the horrors that took place there were an example of what would happen to Israel.

- *All of Israel's support system was taken*
- *away. Can we face God without our usual*
- *props—human leaders, false gods, elaborate*
- *worship rituals? When we stand completely*
- *exposed to God, we can more honestly evaluate the quality of our relationship with Him.*

QUESTIONS TO GUIDE YOUR STUDY

1. Like Israel, do we find ourselves in situations that appear unsolvable even if we have a king or some other leader? How can we rely more on God in these situations?

2. Israel's many promises, oaths, and agreements were followed by many lawsuits. Can other people rely on the promises you make? What should you do when you are unable to fulfill your part of an agreement?

3. Why would Baal worshipers have been particularly attentive to the idea that God "showers righteousness" on the people?

HOSEA 11

Hosea's series of judgment oracles are interrupted by the first of two oracles of hope (Hos.

Wicked High Places

Hosea's phrase "high places of wickedness" (Hos. 10:8) was quite accurate. High places were elevated sites, usually found on the top of a hill, where people sacrificed animals, burned incense to their gods, prayed, ate sacrificial meals, and were involved with male or female cultic prostitutes. Most high places were worship sites for Canaanite deities. Two exceptions were the high places at Dan and Bethel where Israel's King Jeroboam I had put two golden calves (1 Kings 12:28–32) to symbolize the Lord.

Shalmaneser V

The "Shalman" named by Hosea (Hos. 10:14) is sometimes identified with the Assyrian king Shalmaneser V (726–722 B.C.). He completed the attack on Samaria begun by his predecessor, Tiglath-Pileser III. In 722 Israel fell to Shalmaneser (2 Kings 17:6), thus ending the Northern Kingdom.

11:1–11; 14:1–8). As Israel listened to Hosea, they learned the nature of God's deep, undying love for His people, a love going beyond all human love.

God's Parental Love for His Child Israel (11:1–7)

Hosea's preaching described the ups and downs of Israel's relationship to God in family terms. This brief account of Israel's beginnings emphasizes God's love for them—the love of a parent for a child. God called His son Israel, taught him to walk, healed him, fed him, and guided him with kindness. Yet the child did not return the parent's tender love, chasing instead after the Baals.

Israel's rejection of God's love in the past brought them to their current situation. After Assyria's King Tiglath-Pileser died in 727 B.C., Israel's King Hoshea withheld the tribute he had been paying to Assyria. Apparently, Hoshea was encouraged by "So king of Egypt" (2 Kings 17:3–4). This "return to Egypt" for support failed, and in 725 B.C. Assyria's King Shalmaneser V began a campaign against Hoshea's Israel.

Rejecting the tender love of God, Israel was forced to submit to the harsh rule of Assyria as a result of their rebellion. Egypt failed them at a time when God would have saved them.

God's Love Will Not Give Up on His People (11:8–11)

Hosea could be called the "book of God's passion." Divine passion is expressed most graphically as God looks toward Israel's future. In Abraham's day, God had destroyed Admah and Zeboiim, the cities of the plain, along with Sodom and Gomorrah. He could not stand to treat Israel, the people He loved, like He had treated those cities, even though Israel's behavior was bad.

According to the Law of Moses, a stubborn, disobedient son was to be stoned to death (Deut. 21:18–21). Yet, as God the husband showed by forgiving His adulterous wife, so does God the parent show the same love to His disobedient son. The divine change of heart is explained by the words, "I am God, and not man—the Holy One among you" (11:9).

Like Admah and Zeboiim

"The whole land will be a burning waste of salt and sulfur—nothing planted, nothing sprouting, no vegetation growing on it. It will be like the destruction of Sodom and Gomorrah, Admah and Zeboiim, which the LORD overthrew in fierce anger" (Deut. 29:23).

The wrath of God is directed consistently toward those who do not follow His will. At the same time, the sovereign God reveals Himself as a loving parent. Without His love, we could not stand before His wrath.

QUESTIONS TO GUIDE YOUR STUDY

1. How does God's declaration: "I am God, and not man," affect the way we define God? Is it possible to describe God in human terms?
2. In what ways could Israel have shown their gratitude for God's care after they came out of Egypt? What steps might we follow to thank God for His daily loving care?
3. What is the primary purpose of God's discipline in our lives?

HOSEA 12

Israel's Deception and Lies (11:12–12:1)

The last verse of chapter 11 provides the subject matter of chapter 12. Though Judah is mentioned, the focus is on Israel's (Ephraim's)

Chasing the Wind

Wind was a symbol of transience. Ancient writers used the expression "to chase the wind" to represent fruitless striving after an impossible goal. For example, the Preacher of Ecclesiastes described chasing after the wind as "meaningless" (Eccl. 1:14). Hosea considered Ephraim's (Israel's) foreign policy with Assyria and Egypt to be just as futile (Hos. 12:1).

deception of God. They had betrayed God through their covenant making with foreign powers. King Hoshea's attempt to break his vassal treaty with Assyria by seeking support from Egypt was as futile and senseless as trying to catch the wind. It was also an example of the lies and deceit with which Israel deceived the Lord.

Illustrations of Deception (12:2–6)

God's charge against His people is illustrated from stories about the patriarch Jacob. The deeds of Jacob build the case against Israel, showing their deceptive character—like father, like son. A life of deceit began with Jacob's grasping Esau's heel at birth (Gen. 25:26) and continued with Jacob's struggle to overpower God (Gen. 32:24–30). Deceit continues at the site of Bethel, which Jacob founded and Israel had corrupted (Gen. 28:10–22; 35:1–7).

Fleeing Like Jacob

Jacob's life was a story of conflict. He always seemed to be running from someone or something—from Esau, from Laban, or from famine in Canaan (Hos. 12:12). His life, like ours, was a checkered history of rebellion and flight. What raised Jacob above himself was his longing for the salvation of God. Such longing can lift us, too, above our conflicts.

Israel's benefit in reviewing stories of their ancestor Jacob is expressed in the command, "Return to your God" (12:6). Hope for Israel's future lay in their repentance and God's forgiveness and love. The loving God was willing to restore their relationship, as He is ours.

Evidence of Deception (12:7–14)

The charge against Israel builds with other evidence of their deceit and lies. They are as deceptive as Canaanite merchants who suppose that their wealth and success will hide their dishonest tactics. God delivered Israel from Egypt and guided them through His prophets; still, Israel turned to wickedness and idolatry, as proven by deeds at Gilead and Gilgal (12:9–11).

Finally, sentence is pronounced upon Israel. At the cultic site of Bethel they had identified with their ancestor Jacob. The deceptive patriarch who was forced to flee Canaan and serve in a foreign country to obtain a wife should not have been Israel's model. Israel rejected a better model—the Lord, who through His prophet Moses cared for them. For Israel's contempt of God, they must bear guilt.

QUESTIONS TO GUIDE YOUR STUDY

1. Hosea's instruction was to "maintain love and justice" (12:6). How can we show love to evildoers while also seeking justice against the evil they do?

2. Wealth and success are often valued more today than the method by which they are achieved. Do we think that our wealth will hide any sin committed to attain it? Which is more important to us—our integrity or the bottom line?

3. In the web of conflict and tragedy surrounding the patriarch Jacob's life, God's hand was guiding, though hidden. How can you find God working underneath the raging conflicts in your own life?

HOSEA 13

Chapter 13 pronounces the verdict against Israel—a verdict of death. These oracles of judgment possibly relate to events during the last days of Samaria. The question "Where is your king?" (13:10) suggests a date around 725 B.C. when Assyria's Shalmaneser V imprisoned King Hoshea (2 Kings 17:4).

Disappearing Dew

Moist air from the Mediterranean Sea is largely responsible for the dewfall in western Palestine. Moisture forms into drops of water upon the earth during a cool night. While the dew is refreshing, it quickly evaporates under the heat of the sun. For Hosea, the disappearing dew symbolized Israel's coming judgment; they would disappear as a nation as quickly as the early dew (Hos. 13:3).

The Decline of Ephraim (13:1–3)

Hosea usually applied the term "Ephraim" to all of Israel. To show Israel how they had declined, Hosea reminded them of when the tribe of Ephraim was the leading tribe of the Northern Kingdom. That Ephraim was "exalted," but the current Ephraim (all of Israel) was dead because of Baal worship.

Just how far Israel had departed from God is shown by their conduct. They "sin more and more" and even "kiss the calf-idols" (13:2). The kiss was a gesture of extraordinary reverence to idols (1 Kings 19:18). Various images—mist, dew, chaff, smoke—show how transitory their status is. Israel is a dead nation with no future.

Their Savior Becomes a Lion (13:4–11)

Hosea offers two remarkably different pictures of God. One is God the Savior, who brought Israel out of Egypt and cared for them in the desert. The second is God the Lion, who will attack and devour them.

Israel's Sentence of Death (13:12–16)

The prophet made his last announcement of judgment. What is clear is that Israel cannot escape punishment; their guilt is on record and God will not forget their evil deeds. The time for repenting and returning to God has arrived, but they do not know it. Like a child who will not leave the womb, Israel will not accept new life from God (13:13).

Hosea offered one last glimpse of hope. God has power over the death and the grave and is capable of ransoming souls from its depths (13:14). Israel's true helper can save them from death's destruction if they will return to Him. But they will not. The final picture of approaching judgment is grim as it focuses on the plight of

Samaria, the capital city. When the "east wind" comes (representing the Assyrian army), every individual in the city will fall.

One way of resisting God is for a person to harden his or her heart. A stubborn attitude can become a consistent pattern of rejecting God's will. We must stay spiritually aware, lest we allow our hearts to harden to the point that we no longer recognize the time for returning to God.

O Death!

"'Where, O death, is your victory? Where, O death, is your sting?' The sting of death is sin, and the power of sin is the law. But thanks be to God! He gives us the victory through our Lord Jesus Christ" (1 Cor. 15:55–57).

QUESTIONS TO GUIDE YOUR STUDY

1. The history of Ephraim declined from an exalted tribe to an idolatrous nation. Can you look back upon a time in the past when your relationship with God was closer than it is now?

2. Once Israel was satisfied with their lives, they forgot God. Is it easier to rely on God when things are going good or when they are going bad?

3. Do you think that God still keeps our sins "on record" as were Israel's? What is God's solution for our guilt?

HOSEA 14

REPENTANCE RESULTS IN RESTORATION AND LIFE (14:1–9)

Chapter 14 is the second of two oracles of hope that appear among Hosea's series of judgment oracles (see Hos. 11:1–11). Hosea had the task of presiding over the death of his beloved nation, but he held out hope of national revival

Repeated Sacrifices

In the Old Testament, the forgiveness of God was channeled through the sacrificial offerings. Forgiveness was an act of mercy freely bestowed by God, not purchased by the one bringing the offering (Hos. 14:2). Still, the sacrificial system could never give once-for-all forgiveness. The sacrifices had to be repeated over and over. Praise God for the sacrifice Christ provided of Himself once for all (Heb.10:1–4, 10)!

based on radical repentance. After calling Israel to return to their God, the prophet suggests a prayer of penitence (14:2b–3). Linked to that prayer is the Lord's promise of healing for His people (14:4–8).

The Call to Return (14:1–3)

Since coming out of Egypt, God's people had sought forgiveness through the sacrificial system of the covenant relationship which God had established. Hosea now emphasized a new basis for forgiveness—a repentant heart. He was not refuting sacrifices completely, but deepening Israel's understanding of the role of sacrifice. They would still bring an offering to the Lord, showing their sense of need, but they would now offer the fruit of their lips.

- *The Lord was not pleased with the many sac-*
- *rifices that Israel had offered upon their*
- *many altars (Hos. 8:13). Yet, with only their*
- *lips they could offer a sacrifice in which God truly delights. To please God, we must offer Him sacrifices revealing "a broken spirit, a broken and contrite heart" (Ps. 51:16–17).*

The Promise of Healing (14:4–8)

Hosea would not have called on Israel to repent without God's promise of openness toward them. God was standing by, ready to heal, ready to love, ready to offer salvation. Once Israel admitted their waywardness, God was ready to turn away His wrath.

Reconciliation for Israel is described in their renewed fruitfulness. They would blossom, send down roots, and grow up shoots. These images from nature of flourishing vegetation and luxuriant plant growth are Hosea's final statement against the idols of Canaanite fertility religion. Israel had no more need to worship Baal as the provider of fertility. The people's fruitfulness comes from the Lord.

Wisdom to Understand (14:9)

The final verse of the book of Hosea is a wisdom saying that summarizes the prophet's message. Wisdom in the ancient world was the art of learning how to succeed in life and to find the essence of life. Hosea concludes that life's essence is to be found in "the ways of the Lord." The righteous realize this, follow the Lord's ways, and find real life. Those who rebel against His ways, as Israel had, stumble and fall.

A just God must "have no compassion" (Hos. 13:14) on rebellious, stubborn, wayward people. Though He disciplines the sinful, a merciful God is always ready to forgive and restore a penitent, humble people.

QUESTIONS TO GUIDE YOUR STUDY

1. Why did Israel need to see themselves as "fatherless" (14:3) before they could begin a process of genuine repentance?

2. The psalmist declared, "The LORD is good and his love endures forever" (Ps. 100:5). Why is it so important for us to keep in view the permanence of God's love for His people?

3. How does God's offer of forgiveness provide us with a second chance for a renewed life?

The Olive Tree

Olive trees require a Mediterranean type of climate consisting of moist, cool winters and hot, dry summers to be productive. Although flowering begins when the trees are less than ten years old, full yield of fruit is not reached until they are forty or fifty years old, after which branches are pruned to encourage new growth.

Part of the "splendor" of the olive tree (Hos. 14:6) is the varied use of the tree and its fruit. Olive oil was used for cooking purposes as an essential part of the diet. It was rubbed over skin and hair. Medicinally, olive oil mixed with antiseptic wine healed wounds. Taken internally, the oil soothed gastric disorders and acted as a laxative.

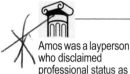

Amos was a layperson who disclaimed professional status as a prophet. As a shepherd, he was "tending the flock" (7:15) when God called him to prophesy.

The listing of Amos as "one of the shepherds of Tekoa" (1:1) may not adequately represent his occupation. In Hebrew, Amos's work as a shepherd is described with the same word used for King Mesha of Moab, who "raised sheep" and supplied Israel's King Ahab with lambs and rams' wool (2 Kings 3:4). So Amos, too, may have been a sheepbreeder rather than a simple shepherd.

Tending the Sycamore Trees

One of Amos's occupations was as a dresser of sycamore-fig trees (Amos 7:14). The tending involved slitting the top of each piece of fruit to hasten its ripening and to produce a sweeter, more edible fruit. Fruit infested with insects might be discarded at this time.

THE BOOK OF AMOS

One might describe the prophet Amos as a "burden bearer." He carried a heavy burden for his people. Or, from another perspective, his people were a burden he carried. Amos ministered as a prophet in Israel shortly before Hosea's ministry there. While Hosea preached judgment with a broken heart, Amos did so with a lion's roar (Amos 1:2).

AUTHOR

From the title verse (1:1) and the narrative of Amos's encounter with the priest Amaziah (7:10–17), we learn more personal information about the man Amos than we know about Hosea, Joel, and Obadiah combined.

According to Amos's own report, his background includes two vocations. Besides a shepherd, he was also a tender of sycamore-fig trees (7:15). This particular tree of the Jordan valley had leaves like a mulberry tree, but the taste of its fruit was inferior to that of an authentic fig tree. Amos was employed to puncture the fruit at a specific time in its growth, making it more edible.

DATE OF WRITING

The time of Amos's ministry is indicated generally by the mention of two kings in the title verse. While King Uzziah was ruling in Judah and King Jeroboam II was ruling in Israel, Amos received a message from God. The exact dates of these kings' reigns are unknown, but a period from approximately 792 to 753 B.C. would cover the period both were sitting on their respective thrones.

A more specific reference to the time of Amos's ministry dates his oracles "two years before the earthquake" (1:1). The precise year of this quake has not been settled to everyone's satisfaction, but the historian Josephus relates it to an event in Uzziah's life around 760 B.C. Amos's ministry is usually dated around 765 to 760 B.C., shortly before Hosea's ministry in Israel.

AUDIENCE

Amos's hometown was Tekoa, a city in the highlands of Judah, south of Bethlehem and Jerusalem. But this Judahite shepherd and tree tender was sent to Bethel to rebuke the Northern Kingdom of Jeroboam II. Bethel was both a royal residence and a prominent, idolatrous worship site in Israel. In addition to Amos's prophetic charges against those who sacrificed there (4:4), he predicted the destruction of the city and its altars (5:5–6).

PURPOSE

Israelite society had experienced the inevitable decay which characterizes misdirected prosperity. Corruption was also generated as a byproduct of Canaanite and Phoenician Baal worship, causing infidelity to the Lord's covenant. Thus, Israel's poor moral condition resulted from corrupt religion and the rampant luxury and self-indulgence of material prosperity.

Amos's purpose was to challenge the superficial qualities of Israel's religious institutions and its perversion of justice. Throughout the land the poor were exploited. The prophet's opposition to moral and religious evils led him to emphasize a primary theme: "Let justice roll on like a river, righteousness like a never-failing stream!" (5:24).

The Earthquake

Josephus reported the earthquake that occurred when King Uzziah contracted leprosy: "A great earthquake shook the ground, and a rent was made in the temple . . . and before the city, at a place called Eroge, half the mountain broke off from the rest on the west, and rolled itself four furlongs, and stood still at the east mountain, till the roads, as well as the king's gardens, were spoiled by the obstruction" (*Antiquities of the Jews*, 9.222–227).

Phoenicia's Baal

The marriage between Israel's King Ahab and Jezebel, daughter of the Phoenician king, brought more to Israel than just a new queen. Along with Jezebel came a new emphasis on Canaanite fertility religions, resulting in 450 prophets of Baal and 400 prophets of Asherah being served at the queen's table (1 Kings 18:19).

STRUCTURE AND CONTENT

The book of Amos divides into two sections. The first section (1:1–6:14) consists of Amos's words, mostly judgment oracles directed against Israel. The second section (7:1–9:15) presents the visions of Amos. Through the visions, Amos received special revelation from God that highlighted the moral and spiritual deficiencies of the people. From the interpretation of the vision experiences, Amos then spoke the words of God, appealing to God's past blessings and future judgment. His preaching aimed to provoke Israel toward social justice and mercy for the disadvantaged.

LITERARY STYLE

Amos employs a variety of literary types. Besides the oracles and visions, the book also contains the narrative report of Amaziah's opposition (7:10–17), as well as three hymn stanzas (4:13; 5:8–9; 9:5–6).

THEOLOGY

Justice for the Community

Justice presupposes God's intention for people to be in community. When some persons become weak with respect to the rest of the community, they are to be strengthened so they can continue to be effective members of the community. Biblical justice restores people to community.

While Hosea condemned apostasy through idolatry, Amos emphasized sins of injustice and oppression. Israel thought they were meeting God's requirements by performing the rituals of the sacrificial system. Amos changed that concept, showing justice to be the central demand on all people who bear the name of God. Without justice, other provisions of the sacrificial system are not acceptable to God.

Israel misunderstood their election as the people of God. They falsely believed that their position as a chosen people would prevent them from coming under judgment. Amos changed that concept, contending that Israel had not been elected to privileged status, but to service.

Israel anticipated the coming day of the Lord as a time of salvation from their enemies. Amos changed that concept, announcing that the day of the Lord would come with destruction and darkness for sinful Israel.

THE MEANING OF AMOS FOR TODAY

God seeks to reestablish in His creation an order where all people receive the benefits of life with Him. He will not tolerate sins of social injustice, but will punish persistent wrongdoers. The church today must seek a faith that cares for the needy groups of society.

AMOS 1

The first section of the book of Amos (Amos 1:1–6:14) consists of the words of the prophet. Amos addressed various issues, but the central theme emphasized sin and judgment. Whether addressing other nations, Israel, or Judah, the prophet confronted and condemned the people's sin.

GOD'S WORD IS REVEALED IN HUMAN WORDS (1:1–2)

The opening verses (1:1–2) provide the historical setting as well as the theme of the book. From the beginning of the book it is clear that Amos speaks for God. Although these prophecies are called "the words of Amos" (1:1), the prophet's words are the medium through which "the LORD roars" (1:2).

The Title of the Book (1:1)

Amos was not a professional prophet on the king's payroll. By his own admission, Amos staked no claim to being a prophet or even being a disciple of a prophet (Amos 7:14).

Zion

"Zion" originally referred to the fortified hill of pre-Israelite Jerusalem, situated between the Kedron and Tyropean valleys. After David captured Zion, he resided there and it became known as the "city of David." Biblical writers used the name "Zion" in a variety of ways. It stood for the capital of Judah (Amos 6:1), for the city of God in the new age (Isa. 1:27; 28:16), and for God's holy hill, on which the Temple was built. Amos spoke of the Lord roaring from this hill (Amos 1:2).

Earthquakes

Palestine has two to three major quakes a century and two to six minor shocks a year. The major quake centers in Palestine are Upper Galilee, near the town of Shechem, and near Lydda on the western edge of the Judean mountains. Both Amos (Amos 1:1) and Zechariah (Zech. 14:5) mention the earthquake that occurred while Uzziah was king.

Rather, Amos was a shepherd, specifically a shepherd from the town of Tekoa. Yet from among the shepherds who worked around Tekoa, God called Amos to preach to the Northern Kingdom of Israel.

The naming of kings Uzziah and Jeroboam II and mention of the earthquake place Amos's ministry some time around 765 to 760 B.C.

■ *Amos was a person dedicated to serving the*
■ *Lord. Yet he was not seminary-trained, was*
■ *not elected to the church board, and was not*
■ *the son of a prominent church family or reli-*
■ *gious official. He was simply a layperson,*
■ *"one of the shepherds." Amos's call was suf-*
■ *ficient credentials for serving God.*

The Theme of the Book (1:2)

Amos concisely stated the theme of the entire book. The message would be one of God's judgment upon His disobedient people. Furthermore, the message originated from Jerusalem—Zion. Although the religious center for the apostate religion of the Northern Kingdom was in Bethel, the people would be confronted by a God who spoke from Zion. They would not answer to the golden calf of Bethel, but to the covenant God of Jerusalem.

If the rejection of Bethel did not capture the people's attention, then Amos's imagery of shepherding would. A shepherd who cared for the welfare of his sheep bristled at the sounds of impending danger. Two such sounds were the roar of a lion and the thunder of an approaching storm.

With these poetic images, Amos described the awesome presence of God, who would manifest Himself through catastrophic force. The whole land, from the pastures to the top of Mount Carmel, would experience divine devastation. This prophet's message was not for the fainthearted.

GOD'S JUDGMENT AGAINST THE NATIONS (1:3–2:16)

Amos condemned those who sinned against a universal conscience (1:1–2:3), against God's revealed law (2:4–5), or against God's redeeming love (2:6–16). The condemnations are presented in the form of eight oracles of judgment.

Oracle Against Damascus (1:3–5)

The first oracle displays the form of a messenger speech, a form followed by the other oracles as well. All eight oracles begin with an introductory messenger formula: "This is what the LORD says" (1:3, 6, 9). Most of the oracles close with a concluding messenger formula: "Says the LORD" (1:5). These formulas focus God's judging and ruling activities on the single concept of His divine authority as Sovereign over all nations. He renders righteous verdicts based upon His divine will.

Another element common to all eight oracles is the graduated numerical saying, "For three sins of . . . even for four" (1:3, 6, 9). Number symbolism was widespread in the biblical world. Three as a symbolic number often indicated completeness. Four was often used as a sacred number. Possibly Amos's numerical saying emphasizes the "fullness" of the people's sins. God had been patient with their sinful ways, but Amos announces divine patience had reached its limit. Judgment would now fall.

Damascus was the capital of the important city-state of Aram (1:3, 5). Situated northeast of

Poetry and Images

Hebrew writers of poetry knew how to combine words to produce brilliant effects. Amos used words to convey the awesome power and force of the Lord who "roars" and "thunders" (Amos 1:2). The prophet also chose words like "dry up" and "withers" to picture the devastation of God's judgment.

Israel, Aram-Damascus had close historical ties to Israel, but those ties were often characterized by strife and warfare. Border wars frequently broke out between Aram and Israel over Gilead, the north-central section of the Transjordanian highlands.

Philistine Cities

Politically, the Philistines had a highly organized city-state system comprised of five towns in southwest Palestine: Ashdod, Gaza, Ashkelon, Gath, and Ekron. Each of the city-states was ruled by a "lord," a king-like figure. Gath was perhaps the major city of this Pentapolis, serving as the hub of the city-state system.

■ *Spiritual anxiety should arise within us when-*
■ *ever our conduct can be characterized as "three*
■ *sins, even four." Mounting transgressions*
■ *against God's will can become, over time, a*
■ *pattern of continuous sinful living. Let us con-*
■ *fess our sins, seeking God's forgiveness, lest we*
  strain His compassionate patience.

Oracle Against Gaza (1:6–8)

The remaining oracles against various nations follow the same messenger speech form displayed in the oracle against Damascus. What changes is the name of the nation and the description of the specific sin involved.

The condemnation of Gaza is actually a condemnation of the prominent cities of the Philistines. Gaza, Ashdod, Ashkelon, and Ekron all belonged to a league of five Philistine city-states, which banded together and were known as the Pentapolis. The one city not mentioned, Gath, was omitted possibly because King Uzziah of Judah had partially destroyed it, making it once again a part of Judah's territory (2 Chron. 26:6).

The specific sin of the Philistines was slave trading. Slavery cut across races and nationalities, and people often became slaves as a result of being captured in war. The Philistines had taken "whole communities" captive, selling the victims to Edom. It is not known whether

Edom used the slaves or sold them to other foreign nations.

Oracle Against Tyre (1:9–10)

Tyre was an ancient Phoenician city, founded long before the Israelites entered the land of Canaan. Along with Sidon, the city was known for maritime exploits and as a center for trade. Apparently, one facet of Tyre's trading must have dealt with slaves, for this city is charged with the same sin as Gaza—selling "whole communities" to Edom.

What made Tyre's sin so unjust was the disregard for "a treaty of brotherhood" (1:9). Exactly what constituted this treaty is not known, although a major alliance between Israel and Phoenicia took place a century before Amos's time. About 870 B.C., Israel's King Ahab married Jezebel, the daughter of the Phoenician king. Alliances and treaties between nations were often sealed by such political marriages.

Oracle Against Edom (1:11–12)

The Edom oracle is the first of three oracles (Edom, Ammon, Moab) condemning nations that were ethnically related to Israel. Edomites were descended from Esau, Jacob's brother, while Ammonites and Moabites were descended from Lot, Abraham's nephew.

Enmity between Israel and Edom began with the patriarchal brothers Jacob and Esau. Esau, lacking self-control, sold his birthright to Jacob for food (Gen. 25:30–34), and later Jacob, through deception, stole the blessing that belonged to Esau as the eldest son (Gen. 27:30–38). Years later, the two brothers were reconciled and met again for a final time at the death of their father Isaac (Gen. 35:29). Although their personal hostility was resolved,

Treaty with Tyre

Tyre disregarded a "treaty of brotherhood" (Amos 1:9). Israel had a long history of treaties with Tyre. King David employed Tyrian stonemasons and carpenters and used cedars from that area in building a palace (2 Sam. 5:11). The construction of the Temple in Jerusalem during Solomon's reign depended heavily on materials and craftsmen from Tyre (1 Kings 5:10–11).

their descendants continued to struggle against one another for centuries.

Oracle Against Ammon (1:13–15)

Rabbah of Ammon

Rabbah was the capital of Ammon, located about twenty-three miles east of the Jordan River. King David captured the city, and it remained under Israelite control throughout the period of the United Monarchy. After Israel and Judah divided, Rabbah regained its independence.

The Israelites recognized the Ammonites as relatives, although somewhat more distant than the Edomites. Specifically, the Ammonites were said to have descended from an ancestor named Ben Ammi, one of two sons which Lot bore to his two daughters.

The kingdom of Ammon, located on the eastern fringe of Gilead, was destined to be a constant enemy of the Israelites. Ammon's proximity to the fertile Gilead resulted in frequent battles with Israel for possession of the area. The charge against the Ammonites that they "ripped open the pregnant women of Gilead" (1:13) seems evil and demented. Nevertheless, such violence was commonly used in border wars to terrorize and demoralize the opponent (2 Kings 15:16).

■ *The Ammonites were willing to murder*
■ *defenseless women in order to enlarge the*
■ *borders of their territory. We wonder how*
■ *humans can have so little regard for human*
■ *life and can commit such brutal deeds for the*
■ *sake of wealth and possessions. Although our*
■ *misdeeds are much less brutal, do we also*
■ *value materialistic gain above the sacredness*
■ *of human life?*

QUESTIONS TO GUIDE YOUR STUDY

1. How long should God remain patient to allow sinners the opportunity to repent? What circumstances call for God to end His longsuffering and execute judgment?

2. What "law of God" had the foreign nations violated?

3. When we choose to become part of a community relationship, such as a "brotherhood" or "sisterhood," what responsibilities and obligations to others in the community do we take upon ourselves?

AMOS 2

Amos's Israelite listeners probably were not disturbed by condemnations proclaimed against other nations, even Edom and Ammon. But the oracles of judgment now moved closer to Amos's intended audience. Following oracles against Moab (2:1–3) and Judah (2:4–5), Amos would indict Israel (2:6–16).

Oracle Against Moab (2:1–3)

Moab's sin was not against Israel at all, but against Edom. The exact nature of the crime, described as burning the bones of Edom's king, is uncertain. Did Moab burn the king to death, or did they burn the bones of a dead king? The expression "burning to lime" indicated complete annihilation, since lime could be obtained only by using high temperatures.

Oracle Against Judah (2:4–5)

All of Amos's first six judgment oracles had charged the guilty nations with war crimes. Their sins were crimes against humanity. Judah's sin, however, concerned the covenant. Judah had rejected "the law of the LORD" (2:4).

Making covenants with His people characterized God, distinguishing Him from the other gods of the nations. Judah's and Israel's God was

The history of the Moabites was intertwined with that of Israel. Moreover, the Moabites were close relatives of Israel, being descended from the son Moab whom Lot bore to one of his two daughters (Gen. 19:36–37).

the one "who keeps his covenant of love with those who love him and obey his commands" (Neh. 1:5). Sadly, Judah did not mirror God's faithfulness to the covenant. The Israelites in Amos's audience were possibly squirming under Judah's condemnation, for their sins also fell short of covenant obedience.

- *In one sense Judah's sin was more serious*
- *than the sins of the foreign nations. Judah*
- *had what the other nations lacked—a cove-*
- *nant with God. When we know God's will,*
- *yet reject it, we bear greater guilt than those*
- *who have had less revealed to them.*

Oracle Against Israel (2:6–16)

The Israelites probably listened intently as Amos uttered oracles of condemnation against their neighbor nations: "For three sins of Damascus ... of Gaza ... of Tyre, Edom, Ammon, Moab, and even Judah." What did the Israelites think as they heard Amos condemn Judah, his own nation, for covenant disobedience? The bigger question, though, was how would the Israelites react when Amos added their name to the formula: "For three sins of *Israel*"?

Israel deserves judgment (2:6–8). While Amos had indicted each of the previous nations with one specific charge, with Israel he had much more to discuss. The several sins charged against Israel concerned the perversion of justice.

Justice involves enabling or allowing all members of a community to participate in aspects of the life of that community. Oppression causes

Breaking the Covenant

David's son Solomon blazed the trail of covenant breaking, worshiping other gods and setting an example that Israel consistently followed through its history (1 Kings 11:11). Covenant violations in Israel became so extreme that a lonely, persecuted prophet could claim, "I am the only one left, and now they are trying to kill me too" (1 Kings 19:10). Judah's failure to keep the covenant (Amos 2:4) continued a pattern begun centuries before.

injustice, for to oppress is to use power for one's own advantage while depriving others of their basic rights in the community. The sin of Israel was denying justice to the oppressed (2:7).

Oppression in Israel occurred in several forms. "Righteous," innocent people were sold for silver, either into slavery or in court by bribing corrupt judges (2:6). Both father and son profaned God's holy name by sleeping with the same woman (2:7). Debtors did not receive back their pledged garments, also a covenant violation (2:8). The poor were required to pay unjust fines, which were paid in wine (2:8).

Israel rejects God's actions (2:9–12). What made Israel's sinful actions so inexcusable were the redeeming actions of God on Israel's behalf. The nation owed its very existence to God's saving works.

Amos's list of God's works contrasts sharply with Israel's oppressive ways. The first work, destruction of the Amorites (2:9), made it possible for Israel to enter the land of Canaan. The term *Amorite* is used often as a general name for all the inhabitants of Canaan, much like the term *Canaanite*. Amorites were a formidable obstacle to the Israelites' conquest and settlement of Canaan. One example of God's mighty work was the victory He orchestrated for Joshua's army over five Amorite kings (Josh. 10:5–15).

A most important event in which God acted redemptively was Israel's escape from slavery in Egypt (2:10). This deliverance was followed immediately by God's preservation of the escaping Hebrews as they wandered for forty years through a "vast and dreadful desert" (Deut. 1:19). Israel had celebrated these events in its

Removing the Sandal

One charge against Israel was the selling of "the needy for a pair of sandals" (Amos 2:6). In early Israel, legal contracts and oaths were often sealed with the removal and giving of a shoe by one party (Ruth 4:7). Possibly the violation Amos had in mind involved selling the needy into slavery in exchange for property.

creeds (Deut. 26:5–9) and sang about them in worship (Ps. 78), yet the nation must now be reminded of them by Amos.

Besides the unique saving events, God also provided Israel with spiritual leaders, who offered guidance across the years. The prophets influenced almost every institution of Israel, despite often being viewed with contempt. Nazirites were lifelong members of a class which served as models of devotion to God.

God had dealt with Israel in a special, unique way throughout its history. No other nation had experienced God's care and provision as had Israel. As part of the indictment against the Israelites, they must acknowledge God's activity on their behalf: "Is this not true, people of Israel?" (2:11). Sadly, they had abused their privileged position, corrupting both prophets and Nazirites (2:12).

God announces judgment (2:13–16). Israel would feel the crushing weight of God's judgment. In a description of complete devastation, expressed in the language of military warfare, Amos warned that Israel's past deliverances would be replaced by defeat.

Nazirite Signs

Amos shows an ethical concern for protecting the status of the Nazirite (Amos 2:12). Nazirites maintained certain outward signs to illustrate their devotion to God, such as the growth of hair, abstention from wine, and avoidance of contact with the dead. Violations of these signs resulted in defilement and the need for purification.

When we contemplate all of the spiritual blessings and advantages Israel had that other nations lacked, we marvel that the Israelites strayed so far from God. How could they forget what God had done for them? Yet we today also forget at times how faithful God has been to us.

QUESTIONS TO GUIDE YOUR STUDY

1. As Christians, what spiritual experiences have we had that make us more accountable for the way we conduct our daily lives?

2. At various points in life we cross paths with persons who are needy or disadvantaged. Do we make personal sacrifices to help them in their need, or do we take advantage of their helplessness for our own personal benefit?

3. What gracious deeds has God performed on your behalf? How have you responded to God as a result?

AMOS 3

PUNISHMENT FOR ISRAEL (3:1–15))

Amos introduces the first of three judgment oracles against Israel, each of which begins with the formula, "Hear this word" (3:1; 4:1; 5:1). He challenged the people to live by covenant standards and condemned them for their failure to reflect the covenant in daily life. Because the Lord had a unique relationship with Israel, He must now punish His people, for they "do not know how to do right" (3:10).

Privilege Brings Responsibility (3:1–2)

Amos's opening call, "Hear this word," sounded like a wisdom teacher preparing his audience to hear a proverb: "Now then, my sons, listen to me" (Prov. 8:32). The message to follow indeed would be instructive, but it would also outweigh any proverb in importance. Its intended audience was not just Israel, the Northern Kingdom, but Israel, "the whole family," whom God had redeemed from Egyptian slavery.

A Chosen People

"For you are a people holy to the LORD your God. The LORD your God has chosen you out of all the peoples on the face of the earth to be his people, his treasured possession" (Deut. 7:6).

The Israelites would not have been surprised when Amos said, "You only" (3:2). They knew that out of all the peoples on earth God had chosen to reveal Himself in a unique way to one particular people. They had been elected to be God's people.

Israel's election may have involved certain privileges, but it also involved greater responsibilities and accountability. Because Israel had failed to maintain their part of this unique relationship, punishment would come.

■ *Israel had not done anything to earn its priv-*
■ *ileged relationship with God. The nation did*
■ *not "deserve" to be chosen. How often do we*
■ *reflect on our own salvation experience and*
■ *remember that the spiritual blessings we*
■ *enjoy are not ours "by right." Rather, God*
■ *wants us to be His people, and for that we*
■ *should be appreciative and thankful, not*
■ *proud and assuming.*

God Speaks to His Prophets (3:3–8)

Each of the rhetorical questions in 3:3–6 links a particular effect to its corresponding cause. People journey together only if they have made prior arrangements. Lions roar only when they have prey. A capture occurs only when birds and traps are present. People tremble when they hear the trumpet's warning blast.

To authenticate his prophetic ministry, Amos announced a spiritual cause and effect, establishing a relation between God's will and what happens in history. This cause/effect principle presumes God's sovereignty over all history. When God speaks, His prophet must prophesy.

When the prophet thus announces judgment, disaster will come (3:6–8).

God Uses Agents in His Judgment (3:9–12)

The sovereign God exercises His lordship over the world by working in His world. He accomplishes His eternal purposes through peoples of the world. Preparing for Israel's judgment, God calls on Ashdod and Egypt to serve as witnesses to Israel's sins of oppression. He has had enough of Israel's infidelities and rebellions; thus, He will call on an enemy to execute His judgment by invading the land.

God Condemns Empty Religion (3:13–15)

The judgment oracle closes with an epilogue that reemphasizes the theme of punishment. Unnamed witnesses are called to testify against the "house of Jacob," a title for Israel that highlights the nation's covenant relationship with God. The covenant between God and the patriarch Jacob had once been renewed at the site of Bethel (Gen. 28:20–22). But now Jacob's descendants had violated that covenant.

From the time of Abraham to the judges, Bethel had been a place of orthodox worship. Israel's King Jeroboam I had corrupted the site, erecting a golden calf and establishing non-Levitical priests, as well as establishing an illegitimate religious feast to compete with the celebrations in Jerusalem. Amos predicted the destruction of this center of idolatry.

Samaria was the capital of the Northern Kingdom as well as the residence and burial place of Israel's kings. King Ahab's palace in Samaria had been decorated with ivory panels, some of which have been recovered by archaeologists (1 Kings 22:39). The rich patrons of the city had built great mansions, at the expense of the poor.

The Lord Caused It

The people wondered why they had to suffer invasions and destruction from their enemies. Amos taught that these disasters fell upon their cities because "the LORD caused it" (Amos 3:6). The source of their troubles was the Lord's decisions. The sovereign God will accomplish His will in His world, and we must accept His will even when He requires punishment for our sin.

Bringing Back the Bones

Shepherds would recover bones of a sheep that was killed by a wild animal as proof to the owner that they had not allowed the sheep to be stolen (Amos 3:12). The Law of Moses specified: "But if the animal was stolen from the neighbor, he must make restitution to the owner. If it was torn to pieces by a wild animal, he shall bring in the remains as evidence and he will not be required to pay for the torn animal" (Exod. 22:12–13).

Samaria Falls!

Samaria fell to the Assyrian armies in 722 B.C. after a three-year siege (2 Kings 18:9–10). King Ahab's ivory house, which he built for Jezebel, was turned to rubble. This destruction came after many prophecies concerning Samaria's sins and many warnings about its doom (Amos 3:15).

Such splendor brought pride to the citizens of Samaria, but Amos announced the doom of these great houses (Amos 5:11; 6:4, 11).

- *At Bethel, the Israelite worshipers engaged*
- *in religious rituals and considered them-*
- *selves to be quite "religious." Yet they failed*
- *to distinguish between religious activities*
- *and true religion.*

QUESTIONS TO GUIDE YOUR STUDY

1. What has God revealed to us as Christians that makes us more accountable than non-Christians to live a life of faithfulness to God?

2. How are God's warnings to us concerning sin actually an aspect of His mercy?

3. What spiritual problems might result in people "not knowing how to do right"? What spiritual safeguards should we Christians enact today to ensure that we always remember what it is to "do right"?

AMOS 4

PREPARE TO MEET GOD (4:1–13)

In a second oracle beginning with the call "Hear this word" (see 3:1; 5:1), Amos continued warning Israel of God's impending judgment. His condemnations focused on the wealthy women of Samaria (4:1–3) and on the idolatrous worship centers at Bethel and Gilgal (4:4–5).

Insatiable Desire of Samaria's Women (4:1–3)

Judgment would be severe for the "first ladies of Samaria," who encouraged violence and injustice on the part of their husbands. As court officials, the husbands used power to exploit the poor in an effort to satisfy and support the lifestyle of their demanding, indulgent wives. No wonder Amos described the women as "cows of Bashan" (4:1).

Empty, Meaningless Worship (4:4–5)

Bethel had been the site of idolatrous worship since the reign of Jeroboam I (930–909 B.C.). Much earlier than that, when Joshua led the conquest of Canaan, Gilgal was the first foothold on Palestinian soil; it also became Israel's first worship place. The charge against Israel concerned not the particular rituals followed at these sites but the attitude of worship. "Bragging" and "boasting" about one's religious activities hardly suggests the demeanor of a reverent, grateful worshiper.

Stubbornness Rather Than Repentance (4:6–11)

A series of five judgments (4:6–11) reveals Israel's stubborn refusal to repent. The calamities that the Lord inflicted—famine, drought, plant disease, plague, wars, and destruction—were intended to bring Israel to repentance. Amos closed each judgment with the oracle formula, "Declares the Lord" and with the refrain, "Yet you have not returned to me" (4:6, 8).

Bringing the Tithes

The Israelites brought tithes "every three years" (Amos 4:4) in accordance with the Law of Moses: "At the end of every three years, bring all the tithes of that year's produce and store it in your towns" (Deut. 14:28). The Deuteronomic code stipulated that this third year's tithe was for the care of the Levites, orphans, widows, and foreigners.

The Bread of Thanksgiving

The fellowship offering was a "sacrifice of thanksgiving," to be accompanied by cakes of both leavened and unleavened bread (Lev. 7:11–13). Amos's listeners were bringing bread with their thank offerings (Amos 4:5), as prescribed by the law, but they were doing so with a boastful attitude. Genuine thanksgiving should be a natural element of our Christian worship and should characterize all of our Christian life.

- *With divine patience, God withholds judg-*
- *ment to allow His people time to repent. We*
- *must not treat such kindness with contempt,*
- *for one day we will stand before God and*
- *account for our actions (Rom. 2:4–5).*

Meeting God Almighty (4:12–13)

God's rebellious people would now face the ultimate confrontation. They were to prepare for judgment from God Almighty.

The central word in Israel's vocabulary for describing their special relationship with God was *covenant*. The covenant relationship was the basis for God's judgment against Israel. They had been chosen to be God's special people, and so Amos commanded them, "Prepare to meet *your* God, O Israel" (4:12).

Our Creator and God

As Amos announced God's appearance to Israel in judgment (Amos 4:12), he paused to interject a hymn (4:13) reflecting on the Lord God Almighty as the Creator. Christians today should follow Amos's example. Pause a moment from your many church activities, rituals, and programs and worship your God, the Creator of the universe. Nothing in His creation is hidden from His presence. He is worthy of our praise and worship.

The final verse of the chapter is a hymn fragment, the first of three hymns in the book (see 5:8–9; 9:5–6). A hymn expresses a congregation's praise of God's greatness and majesty. The hymn at the end of Amos's oracle expresses the nature of the God who would execute His judgment upon Israel.

- *The Assyrian invasion and destruction that*
- *Israel would suffer was due to God's deci-*
- *sion. The Lord God Almighty said, "This is*
- *what I will do to you, Israel." When God's*
- *people plunge into sin and then refuse to*
- *repent, God must respond in a manner con-*
- *sistent with His character as a holy God who*
- *cannot tolerate sin.*

QUESTIONS TO GUIDE YOUR STUDY

1. To what lengths are you willing to go in order to satisfy your personal needs and desires? Would you oppress another person if such action would get you what you want?

2. Obtaining wealth is not in itself sinful, but how should we allow God to guide the process by which we obtain wealth?

3. What does God do to honor His covenant promise to us? What must we do to honor our covenant promises to Him?

AMOS 5

In the final oracle beginning with the call "Hear this word" (see 3:1; 4:1), Amos proclaimed that the nation was already dead. One could sing Israel's funeral lament, "Fallen is Virgin Israel, never to rise again" (5:2). The theme of lament for Israel's fall continues with two woe oracles, both beginning with the cry, "Woe to you" (5:18; 6:1).

FUNERAL LAMENT FOR ISRAEL (5:1–17)

Amos described the "word" he now offered to Israel as a "lament" (5:1). Loud lamentation was a customary feature of mourning for the deceased. Not only did the actual relatives mourn, but professional mourners were hired as well. The funeral lament consists of seven stanzas: two stanzas each of lamentation, exhortation, and accusation revolve around a hymn stanza.

Lamentation (5:1–3)

The prosperous nation to which Amos prophesied was probably puzzled to hear him pronounce a lament over them. They were blind

The Poetry of Lament

Laments are a unique form of Hebrew poetry. They are elegies or mournful poems which lament some great loss. They are divided into stanzas, as is most poetry. Stanzas are units of poetry lines that express similar thoughts.

Amos's lament (Amos 5:1–16) has an orderly arrangement of stanzas. The first three stanzas present three themes: lamentation, exhortation, and accusation. Then comes a hymn stanza, after which are three final stanzas reversing the order of themes: accusation, exhortation, lamentation.

to the sad truth. Because of their injustice and failure to bind authentic religious experience with a social conscience, the covenant relationship between them and their God had died a painful death.

Exhortation (5:4–6)

In one last attempt to persuade Israel to repent, the Lord exhorted the Israelites, addressed as "the house of Joseph," to seek their God. If they would do so, they must reject the cult centers of Bethel and Gilgal. Bethel had been a place of orthodox worship from the time of the patriarch Abraham to the judges, but Jeroboam I had turned it into the center of his apostate religion. Gilgal was a major place of worship for Israel, but it also featured worship associated with other gods. Both sites were targeted for destruction.

Beersheba, in southern Judah, had strong patriarchal links. Abraham named the place after sealing a treaty there with Abimelech, king of Gerar (Gen. 21:31–32). The Lord confirmed His promises with Isaac at Beersheba (Gen. 26:23–25). Jacob stopped there on his way to Egypt (Gen. 46:1–4). Because of these patriarchal events, Beersheba eventually became a pilgrimage destination for idolatry. Israel must not continue to journey there if they were to seek God.

Accusation (5:7)

In two brief poetic lines, Amos summarized Israel's covenant-breaking behavior: they had perverted justice and righteousness in their society. Righteousness is the fulfillment of the terms of a covenant between God and humanity or between humans in the full range of human relationships. Israel's trampling of righteousness ensured that judgment would come.

Hymn (5:8–9)

The second hymn of the book, like the other two (see 4:13; 9:5–6), magnifies God as the Creator and the controller of creation. In His creative sovereignty, God, who is the source of all things, guides His creation to a meaningful end. That end might mean destruction for those who pervert the justice that God desires for a meaningful society.

Accusation (5:10–13)

Amos continued the charge of perverting justice against Israel by focusing on the corruption of the judicial system. By judging justly the courts could teach God's law and the principles of divine justice. Whenever they recognized the person in the right and imposed an appropriate penalty on the guilty one, they were restoring the community to peace and wholeness under God. In Israel, the system no longer functioned as it should.

A prime concern for Amos was the absence of due process in Israel's court system, as prescribed in the law (Deut. 16:18–20). The plaintiff who "reproves in court" and the witness who testifies truthfully found themselves unwanted. Taking bribes and abusing the poor were popular. This perverted court system was characterized by two differing types of persons. Wealthy landowners manipulated the system for personal advantage, forcing the poor to pay fines or taxes of grain and wine. On the other hand, prudent individuals were wise enough to keep quiet, for the unjust system made for evil situations that were best avoided.

Pleiades and Orion

Orion is a constellation bearing the name of a giant Greek hunter, who, according to myth, was bound and placed in the heavens. Pleiades is a brilliant grouping of seven stars located in the shoulder of the constellation Taurus, named after the seven daughters of Atlas. Amos praised the Lord as the Creator of these heavenly bodies (Amos 5:8).

Righteousness

Righteousness is a faithful fulfillment of the provisions of the covenant. It is living according to God's law which finds fulfillment in love to God and neighbor. All of the religious activity at Bethel, Gilgal, or Beersheba was nothing but empty motions to God while justice and righteousness were denied to the poor. We must not search our hearts only while we are in church, but also while in the home, workplace, and market. Do all of our actions please God?

The Court System

In ancient courts there were no prosecutors or defense attorneys; accuser and accused argued their own cases. The burden of proof lay with the defendant, and proving one's case depended primarily on testimony and persuasive argument. Such a system of justice depended on the honesty of witnesses and the integrity of judges. No wonder Amos condemned corrupt judges and those who supported them (Amos 5:12).

■ *A nation that claims to be "Christian"*
■ *should demonstrate the truth of that claim in*
■ *its public justice system. Are the laws and*
■ *business practices of that nation pleasing to*
■ *God? We should use our influence as Chris-*
■ *tians to encourage the nation's leaders to*
■ *seek justice.*

Exhortation (5:14–15)

The first exhortation urged Israel to "seek the LORD" (5:4, 6); the second urged them to "seek good." Those who would seek God must also pursue what pleases God. In Amos's message seeking "good" meant to seek "justice in the courts" (5:15). Seeking good would not be accomplished by following religious rituals, but by establishing just relationships, especially with the poor.

Lamentation (5:16–17)

The funeral lament, which opened with a lament stanza (5:1–3), also closed with one. The weeping of lamentation would be widespread, through streets, public square, and vineyards.

The Day of the Lord (5:18–20)

With two woe oracles (5:18; 6:1), Amos mourned for Israel. These "woes" are covenant curses. Near Eastern covenants typically included a list of curses that would be brought on by violating the covenant. God recognized that His covenant with Israel had been broken and was thus no longer valid. The prophet must cry, "Woe to you."

The Israelites were familiar with the concept of the "day of the LORD." Indeed, they even looked forward to its arrival. It would be a time when

God would reveal His sovereignty over human powers and human existence. Israel expected it to be a day of light and salvation for them.

Amos and other prophets proclaimed a much different "day of the LORD." Audiences must have been shocked to hear the prophets describe the time as a day of darkness and judgment (Zeph. 1:14–18). The Israelites must change their understanding of this day they had longed for; in reality it would be "pitch-dark, without a ray of brightness" (5:20). The day would not bring life, but death.

The Day of the Lord

"Day of the Lord" does not in itself designate the time perspective of the event, whether it is past, present, or future. The "day of the Lord's anger" can describe a past event, such as the fall of Jerusalem (Lam. 2:1). The day of the Lord could describe a present disaster, such as Joel's locust plague (Joel 1:15). Amos painted the day as a future day of darkness and judgment (Amos 5:20).

■ *Religious people face a continuous danger of*
■ *assuming that they are God's "friends." A*
■ *relationship with God is not to be taken for*
■ *granted, for sinful, disobedient behavior is*
■ *displeasing to a holy God. Let us be religious,*
■ *but let us also do spiritual checkups on our*
■ *souls.*

Sacrifice Without Justice (5:21–27)

Israel had based their hopes of salvation on two things: the day of the Lord and their system of religious sacrifices. They had just received bad news about the day of the Lord; Amos now rejected each feature of their sacrificial worship.

Feasts, assemblies, offerings, and songs in their rituals made it evident that the Israelites were religious people. Yet God wanted to see justice and righteousness in their society to make it evident that they were His people. Without the latter, He would not accept the former.

God reminded Israel that they had enjoyed a close relationship with Him for "forty years in

Stars and the Gods

Amos condemned Israel for becoming involved in Assyrian idolatry by lifting up "the star of your god" (Amos 5:26). He was attacking the Assyrian blend of astrology and religion which believed in links between the movement of stars and events on earth. Assyrians attempted to determine the future by reading the stars to discover proper times for action, and apparently Israel was trying this too.

the desert," even without having a highly developed sacrificial system at that time (5:25). In contrast, their elaborate religious activities in Amos's day (5:26) actually corrupted their relationship with God. Idolatrous worship involving royal shrines and star deities would lead to certain judgment—"exile beyond Damascus."

■ *If Amos were to examine our religious and*
■ *personal lives, would he find evidence of jus-*
■ *tice and genuine devotion? Our conduct in*
■ *day-to-day affairs outside of the church*
■ *counts as much for "true worship" as do our*
■ *activities within church circles.*

QUESTIONS TO GUIDE YOUR STUDY

1. In what ways can the church help those who are poor and needy (besides just giving money)? How can we as individuals make personal, nonfinancial contributions?

2. What are signs that our claim of God being "with us" is accurate?

3. Is God pleased with the practices of your church? Why? Why not?

The second woe oracle centers on the ruling leaders of Israel as well as Judah (6:1–7). These individuals were "at ease," while an "evil day" was about to fall upon their nations. A judgment oracle (6:8–14) announces that God will not tolerate such self-indulgence.

FALSE SECURITY PRECEDES ULTIMATE DOWNFALL (6:1–7)

Israel's and Judah's leaders believed they were secure. Such confidence was ill-founded, for they would be the "first" to experience judgment (6:7). Amos cried, "Woe to you!"

Preeminence in National Strength (6:1–3)

Complacency had grown because they had placed trust in the wrong things. Their current prosperity had deceived the leaders to believe they would always be prosperous. Being aware of their election as the people of Yahweh, both the Northern and Southern Kingdom considered themselves "the foremost nation" (6:1).

From their respective capitals in Jerusalem (Zion) and Samaria, the leaders probably felt invincible. They were the "notable men" of their cities in whom all the people trusted for leadership. They put off any idea that an "evil day" might come. But Amos invited them to view the fate of the conquered cities around them—Calneh in Syria, Hamath north of Damascus, Gath toward the Mediterranean coast. Israel and Judah would face judgment just as those places had.

Look at Calneh

Calneh was a city in Syria that had suffered conquest by Tiglath-Pileser of Assryia in 738 B.C. Amos invited Israel to view Calneh's fate as a conquered city and see if Israel was really better in any way (Amos 6:2). Similarly, Amos's contemporary Isaiah warned Jerusalem that Calneh (also spelled Calno) was as good as Jerusalem, yet had been defeated (Isa. 10:9).

■ *To place confidence in our own strength is*
■ *foolishness. We should learn from others*
■ *who have turned from trusting in God, only*
■ *to see their self-made defenses crumble.*
■ *What has happened to others can also hap-*
■ *pen to us.*

Indulgence in Luxury (6:4–7)

Nothing was too good for the leaders! They slept on elaborately decorated beds. They feasted on meat and game that others ate only on rare occasions. Their wine consumption knew no moderation. They relaxed during leisure time given to music. All of this was going on while the nation was approaching ruin. God would send these leaders a wake-up call of judgment; their indulgences would not follow them into exile.

PRIDE GOES BEFORE THE FALL (6:8–14)

The only hope for Israel and Judah rested in the renewal of authentic religious experience. Short of that, doom was certain, for God would punish their self-indulgence by military defeat.

The Command to Destroy (6:8–11)

Solemn oaths were binding. Anyone who doubted Amos's prediction of destruction must heed God's oath. Swearing by His holiness (4:2) and by Himself (His own person; 6:8), God Almighty gave His authority to Amos's oracle.

Samaria, the capital city of Israel, could be called the "pride of Jacob" (6:8). Situated on a hill, the site was easily defensible. Twice the enemy nation of Syria had led unsuccessful sieges of the city. Yet at God's command, every house in the city would become rubble, from the great royal houses to the small dwellings of the common person (6:11). The only outlook ten survivors would face was eventual death.

The Absurdity of Pride (6:12–14)

Two rhetorical questions raise absurd situations. Of course, no one would use horses or oxen on rocky crags! That is just how absurd Israel's perversion of justice was.

Lo Debar

Equally absurd was Israel's reliance on their own strength and power. Prior to the delivery of this oracle, Lo Debar and Karnaim had been recaptured from the Arameans by Jeroboam II. Israel boasted of the victory as an indication of their own strength, forgetting that God had blessed the campaign. All boasting would cease when God stirred up Assyria to defeat Israel. Assyria's oppression would extend from Israel's northernmost point, Lebo Hamath, to the valley of the Arabah, its southern border.

Amos took the consonants of the name "Lo Debar" (2 Sam. 9:4) and added new vowels to make the name read "a thing of nought" (Amos 6:13). His play on words reminded Israel that its true strength and greatness were not in its military achievements, but in God who had blessed their efforts. All self-efforts that ignore God are "things of nought."

- *God has given us many physical resources to*
- *make our lives easy and comfortable. When*
- *we use these resources solely for our per-*
- *sonal benefit, ignoring the needs of others,*
- *we miss God's purpose in providing them.*
- *We also move toward allowing resources to*
- *replace God as the center of life.*

QUESTIONS TO GUIDE YOUR STUDY

1. How just are we to the people who depend on our leadership and influence?
2. Has our modern culture developed the attitude that a certain lifestyle is ours by right? Does the prosperity of our nation cause us to assume we are entitled to certain things?

3. Developing personal strengths is wise and admirable. Reflect on your own strong points; how many of them are actually blessings from God?

AMOS 7

· · · ·

The second section of the book of Amos (7:1–9:15) contains the visions of Amos. The visions were central to Amos's call experience and may have been the earliest revelations of God to this prophet. By making Amos aware of the awesome reality of human sin and divine judgment, the visions shaped his prophetic message.

VISIONS OF MERCY AND JUDGMENT (7:1–8:3)

Amos received five visions that portrayed God's reluctance to turn Israel over to their executioners. Two times the sentence of judgment is turned back (7:1–3, 4–6). But finally justice requires punishment, and two visions reveal a holy God who can wait no longer (7:7–9; 8:1–3). The fifth vision is a theophany of God beside the altar (9:1–4).

First Vision: Swarms of Locusts (7:1–3)

As in the book of Joel, the image of a locust plague symbolizes being overwhelmed by a large and powerful army (Joel 2:20). A swarm of locusts can strip a land of all vegetation as it moves across the fields.

Amos was alarmed at the timing of the locusts. The king's share of the harvest had been gathered, but the "second crop" for the people would be lost. Even worse, the later rains of February and March were over, and rarely did rain of any significance fall between then and the early rains of October and November. If the locusts took this crop, there would no moisture to produce another crop for some time.

In the introduction Amos described the vision as "what the Sovereign LORD showed me" (7:1). God Himself was preparing this destructive plague. The prophet's task turned to intercession as Amos prayed that God's word would not come to pass. The concern that Israel (Jacob) was too "small" to survive probably does not refer to size. During Amos's time, Jeroboam II had basically restored the boundaries of David's empire, reaching even into Syria. Israel was "small" in the sense of being helpless against the plague.

In both of the first two visions, God changed His plan after Amos interceded on Israel's behalf. God's relenting reveals the important role intercessory prayer can play in relations between God and people. The God who relents is free to answer prayer and to interact with His people.

Second Vision: Fire (7:4–6)

The second vision Amos received was almost the same as the first. Again the Lord showed Amos a coming judgment; again Amos interceded, arguing that Israel was too small to survive; again God relented. The judgment this time was a fire that apparently symbolized a severe drought. Not only was the land affected, but also the "great deep," which sometimes refers to the waters that feed steams and allow the irrigation of the land (Ezek. 31:4).

The Prayer of Intercession

Intercession is the act of mediating between differing parties, particularly the act of praying to God on behalf of another person. Amos's praying for God's word not to come to pass (Amos 7:2) illustrates how important a prophet's task of intercession could be. As Christians, we should have a list of persons for whom we offer prayers of intercession.

So Small!

Amos pleaded with God to forgive Israel (Jacob), reasoning that the nation was "so small" (Amos 7:2, 5) they could not withstand the judgments of the visions. As a nation, Israel in Amos's time was not small. King Jeroboam II had "recovered for Israel both Damascus and Hamath" (2 Kings 14:28). Before we count heavily on human strengths, we should remember that what is "big" or "strong" in human eyes can be very small in the eyes of God.

■ *God responded to Amos's intercession, and*
■ *Israel was spared the judgments of locusts*
■ *and fire. We must not hesitate to pray for*
■ *others, knowing that God accepts a believer's*
■ *prayers through Christ, the mediator*
■ *between God and humanity. Christ inter-*
■ *cedes for us at God's throne of grace.*

Third Vision: Plumb Line (7:7–9)

The third and fourth visions are different. This time Amos did not intercede; this time God did not relent. The message of these visions is that judgment is certain.

In the third vision Amos saw the Lord holding a plumb line and standing by a wall. The plumb line was a cord with a weight of metal or stone attached to one end. It was held beside a wall during construction to assure vertical accuracy. God would test His people to see if they were "true to plumb."

The test of the plumb line revealed Israel to be out of line. The worship sites, including the high places and sanctuaries (7:9), had become places of sin where false gods were worshiped. This time God was out of patience: "I will spare them no longer" (7:8). Israel's King Jeroboam would feel the wrath of God against the disobedient nation.

The Plumb Line

Amos was shown a vision of a plumb line that God would use to measure Israel (Amos 7:7–8). Another prophet, Isaiah, described God's plumb line: "I will make justice the measuring line and righteousness the plumb line" (Isa. 28:17). Israel had been built straight, but the nation was out of line when God measured it by His standards of righteousness.

■ *Sometimes people try to negotiate with God*
■ *over sin. "If You overlook it this time, Lord,*
■ *I won't do it again." "If my situation was dif-*
■ *ferent, this would not have happened." God*
■ *is patient, but our sinful conduct can exhaust*
■ *His patience so that even the intercession of*
■ *an Amos will not stop judgment.*

Amaziah Confronts Amos (7:10–17)

The narrative of the encounter between Amos and the priest Amaziah at Bethel reveals a conflict of authority. As the presiding priest, Amaziah used his authority to order Amos to stop preaching, claiming he did not have the right to prophesy against King Jeroboam in the king's place of worship. Amos replied, "This is what the LORD says" (7:17). Authority rested not with Amaziah, Jeroboam, or Amos, but in the word from the Lord spoken by His prophet.

Priest to the king (7:10–11). Reporting to Jeroboam, Amaziah accused Amos of leading a conspiracy against Israel's royal house. True, Amos had announced the impending death of Jeroboam II and Israel's exile, and other prophets had predicted a revolt. Yet nothing indicated that Amos was conspiring with anyone.

Priest to the prophet (7:12–13). Amaziah possibly had personal motives for sending Amos away. Bethel was Amaziah's territory, and Amos's presence was causing unrest. In addition to condemning sacrificial rituals at Bethel (4:4), Amos had predicted the destruction of Bethel and its false altars (3:14; 5:5).

Prophet to the priest (7:14–17). Amos's credentials were more impressive than Amaziah was

65

Sycamore-Fig Trees

The sycamore-fig tree that Amos tended (Amos 7:14) has no relation to the American sycamore tree. It bore fruit several times a year and was found in abundance in the foothills between the Philistine coastal plain and the highlands of Judah (2 Chron. 9:27). Poor people used the tree's wood, since it was less expensive than cedar (Isa. 9:10).

aware. Denying any previous prophetic activity, Amos emphasized that in Judah, while he was working with flocks and sycamore-fig trees, God had called him to prophesy, and he had obeyed. That call, which brought Amos to Bethel, was sufficient credentials for him to announce judgment on Amaziah and his family (7:17).

■ *Leaders, like Jeroboam, should strive to*
■ *serve God, who granted them authority to*
■ *govern. Priests and ministers, like Amaziah,*
■ *should serve God, who gave them authority*
■ *to minister. Each of us should concentrate*
■ *more on being accountable to God than on*
■ *exerting authority over others.*

QUESTIONS TO GUIDE YOUR STUDY

1. What are the "plumb lines" that God uses to test His people's devotion today? Would your spiritual life measure "true to plumb"?

2. Amaziah rejected any news that threatened to disturb his position. How do you react to people who suggest changes to your surroundings that upset your established routine?

3. Has God asked you to do anything that you think falls outside your area of expertise?

AMOS 8

The narrative of Amos and Amaziah (7:10–17) seems to interrupt the visions. Actually, the conflict between prophet and priest highlights a serious defect in Israel. The dynamism of personal religious experience had given way to the superficiality of institutional religion. This defect calls for the judgment revealed in the third (7:7–9) and fourth (8:1–3) visions.

Fourth Vision: Basket of Fruit (8:1–3)

Amos had cried out for justice. Amaziah had ordered him not to prophesy any more. Now the Lord vows to spare Israel no longer (8:2).

The fourth vision resembles the third (7:7–9). Instead of a plumb line, this time Amos saw a "basket of ripe fruit," but again he offered no intercession. Ripened fruit indicated the end of the growing season, which in the vision suggests the end for Israel. The nation's overripe, rotten religion was worthless, and it was time for judgment. The single command "Silence!" speaks for the end of God's patience.

ISRAEL'S DESOLATION AND RESTORATION (8:4–9:15)

With the call "Hear this," Amos summoned Israel to consider first the charge against them (8:4–6) and then the judgment they would face (8:7–14). The end of the Northern Kingdom was fulfilled in 722 B.C. (9:1–10), but God's desire to spare some for a future shows His consistent love in fulfilling His promises to David (9:11–15).

Israel's Greedy Merchants (8:4–6)

The charge that Amos put forth is by now familiar: Israel has oppressed the poor and

Ripened Fruit

A basket of ripe fruit (Amos 8:1–2) was a vision that a prophet could easily communicate to the Northern Kingdom. Israel was familiar with the process by which trees reproduce by means of seeds carried in fruit. They considered the process to be part of God's good plan at creation, with "trees bearing fruit with seed in it" (Gen. 1:12). They presented offerings of ripe fruit at the Temple (Neh. 10:35). Thus, Amos's vision of judgment was expressed in a language they could understand.

Different Measures

Israel was constantly warned not to buy with one measure and sell with another: "Differing weights and differing measures—the LORD detests them both" (Prov. 20:10).

Merchants in Israel

With the exception of the period when Solomon was king (1 Kings 10:15, 22), Israel was not known in biblical times as a nation of merchants. References in the Bible to Israelites involved in trade are surprisingly few. Amos's account of merchants (Amos 8:5–6) does not speak well of their business ethics. Besides the abuses Amos mentioned, merchants were also known to hold back grain, driving up prices (Prov. 11:26), and to force fellow Israelites into mortgaging their property in order to buy food (Neh. 5:1–3).

The Nile River

Egypt was unique as an agricultural community in not being dependent on rainfall. The secret was the black silt deposited on the fields by the annual flood caused when the Nile River was swollen by the runoff from the winter rains in Ethiopia. If the winter rains failed, famine would occur. Amos's listeners were familiar with a rising and sinking Nile (Amos 8:8).

needy (see 2:6–7; 4:1; 5:11). One place this sin was particularly apparent was in the marketplace, where greedy merchants took advantage of the people. How easy it was to overlook or ignore the Law of Moses, which stipulated that Israel was not to sell food to the poor at a profit (Lev. 25:35–37).

Merchants observed the holy days, but they were impatient for the new moon, Sabbath, and other observances to end so commerce might resume. But God was also impatient with innocent people being victimized by human greed.

The Lord's Oath (8:7–10)

God Himself took an oath, promising to "never forget" how Israel has sinned (8:7). If they would repent, God would "remember their sins no more" (Jer. 31:34). Since they refused, God declared His determination to punish.

An oath was a formal appeal to God or to sacred objects as a support to fulfill a promise. God appealed to "the Pride of Jacob," swearing to execute judgment. "Pride of Jacob" probably refers to the Lord Himself, since God has sworn by His holiness (4:2) and by Himself, His own person (6:8). Israel should have made God their "pride" instead of relying on themselves and on foreign gods.

The coming judgment is described with language of natural phenomena. The land will tremble, rise and sink like the Nile, and turn to darkness. Prophets often used such imagery of God's judgment (Jer. 4:27–28; Joel 2:10). Feasting and singing would be replaced by mourning and weeping.

A Famine of God's Word (8:11–14)

God is utterly free to be where He wills, though He constantly chooses to be with His people to give them life. One means of God's communication to His people was by His word delivered through His prophets. As part of the judgment upon Israel, God chose to withdraw His word. Amaziah had ordered Amos to prophesy no more (7:12–13); now Israel would experience a famine of the prophetic word.

The famine imagery pictures the distress of lacking communication with God. People will "stagger" everywhere to find God's word, to no avail. Young people, normally the strength of a nation, will faint in thirst for the word. Israel had only themselves to blame, for they had been swearing by gods worshiped at Samaria, Dan, and Beersheba, when they should have been worshiping Yahweh alone.

■ *God's word was available to Israel through*
■ *Amos's preaching as it is to us today through*
■ *the Bible. Let us not commit Israel's sin,*
■ *rejecting God's word when it is near.*

Days Are Coming

The prophets used various phrases to announce God's impending judgment. Amos's prophetic announcement "The days are coming" appears with other prophets, such as Isaiah's "The time will surely come" (Isa. 39:6) and Jeremiah's "The days are coming" (Jer. 7:32).

QUESTIONS TO GUIDE YOUR STUDY

1. Israel's merchants found a self-serving way of blending religious appearances with unethical business practices. In what ways does God influence your use of money? How does money influence your worship of God?

2. The Bible offers much guidance for living. Where do people usually look first for answers to life issues before turning to the Bible?

3. Israel had broken the covenant in two ways: oppressing the poor and worshiping false gods. In what areas of society today do we find people placing their trust in "other gods" while treating fellow humans unjustly?

Amos 9

The final chapter of the book of Amos offers a summary thought on judgment: "Surely the eyes of the Sovereign LORD are on the sinful kingdom" (9:8). The fifth vision (9:1–4) shows judgment to be inescapable. A final hymn (9:5–6) affirms God's power to carry out judgment. The last judgment oracle (9:7–10) confirms that Israel's election as the people of God will not exempt them from judgment. Yet hope was not gone—a few would survive and rebuild the nation (9:11–15).

Vision of the Altar (9:1–4)

In a final vision Amos sees the Lord standing by an altar. Though not identified, the altar was likely located at Bethel, an altar from which Amaziah, as priest of Bethel, had banned Amos (7:13). Bethel was an appropriate setting for the Lord to emphasize the certainty of coming judgment.

The vision made clear two things: the devastation would be total and no one would escape. Any attempt to hide from God was futile. Israel could flee to the top of Mount Carmel or to the bottom of the sea, but God would find them. Even if they could go to the grave or to the heavens, God would still reach them. The wrath of God would extend even into foreign exile.

Sheol, the Grave

The word *Sheol* in Hebrew thought referred to the abode of the dead, the grave. Sheol was considered to be deep within the earth and was entered by crossing a river. With the psalmist, Amos affirmed that God is in Sheol, and it is impossible to hide from Him there (Ps. 139:8; Amos 9:2).

■ *How upsetting is the realization that God's*
■ *judgment and wrath are inescapable? For*
■ *those who have been unfaithful to God, the*
■ *sudden insight into divine punishment is ter-*
■ *rifying, for they did not believe they could*
■ *ever suffer such wrath. The faithful are not*
■ *upset at all.*

Hymn to the Lord Almighty (9:5–6)

After the announcement of inescapable punishment comes a third hymn (see 4:13; 5:8–9) naming and glorifying the Lord as the deity powerful enough to execute judgment. God is sovereign ruler over all earth and heaven; He controls the rainfall upon the land. His qualifications to be judge over all persons are not questioned.

Ruin for the Sinful Kingdom (9:7–10)

The reason judgment cannot be escaped rests in the determination of the Sovereign Lord. His "eyes" (7:8) are upon sinful Israel, and because of what He sees, He has decided on judgment.

Dire news of destruction was tempered by one glimmer of hope. The "sinful kingdom" would be destroyed totally, but the "house of Jacob" would not (7:8). While the nation Israel, the Northern Kingdom, would no longer exist, a remnant of people would survive. Some of Jacob's descendants would preserve God's chosen people.

Grain in the Sieve

A sieve was an instrument used to remove unwanted materials from grain. Small rock particles would remain in the sieve, while the grain passed through. God warned Israel He would place them in a sieve of judgment and none would fall through, for none of them were good grain (Amos 9:9).

■ *God is a loving, holy God. The holy God will*
■ *not and cannot hold back punishment of dis-*
■ *obedient sinners. The loving God desires that*
■ *sinners come to repentance.*

Restoration for a Renewed People (9:11–15)

Amos is a book about the Northern Kingdom. Yet at the end of the book is a prophecy concerning the restoration of the Davidic dynasty. David and his son Solomon had ruled all Israel—north and south. But by Amos's time, "David's fallen tent" consisted of a Northern Kingdom ready to fall and a Southern Kingdom weakened after King Uzziah's death.

In the future, in "that day," circumstances would be brighter. The Davidic dynasty would be restored to rule over a united kingdom, controlling all the nations that once were under David's rule (9:11). God would "build" the house of David.

The last verses of the book predict a time when God would bring back Israel's exiles to live permanently in Palestine. Not only would they live again in "their own land," but that land would be a land of plenty. Crops would be so abundant that no sooner than one crop had been reaped, it would be time to plow the next.

Building David's House

Through Amos, the Lord promised to build the house of David "as it used to be" (Amos 9:11). The words recall a much earlier promise of God to King David through Nathan the prophet: "Your house and your kingdom will endure forever before me" (2 Sam. 7:16).

The ultimate fulfillment of these promises would come in the Messiah, the future David. To James, the brother of Jesus, Amos's words were being fulfilled as Gentiles joined the people of God through Christ (Acts 15:13–18). David's fallen tent continues to be rebuilt each time a person joins Christ's church.

■ *Israel's wealthy citizens had hoarded the*
■ *land's wine for themselves, drinking it by the*
■ *bowlful. Judgment took away their vineyards*
■ *and wine (5:11). In the restored land all will*
■ *drink the wine of overflowing vineyards.*

QUESTIONS TO GUIDE YOUR STUDY

1. When God must render judgment, why is it appropriate that He begin at the altar, the center of a people's religious life? Why should He not start in the street where sinners commit their deeds?

2. Why is the attitude that "disaster will not meet us" so dangerous to our spiritual lives?

3. In what ways does the Messiah fulfill God's promises for a renewed, reunited Davidic kingdom led by a Davidic ruler?

THE BOOK OF JOEL

Containing only seventy-three verses, the book of Joel is one of the shortest in the Old Testament, comprising only three chapters in our English translations.

AUTHOR

Personal information concerning Joel is minimal. He is said to be the son of Pethuel, about whom we know nothing. The title verse of the book does not provide the historical context for the prophet's message. It does confirm, however, that Joel, like Hosea, was a genuine prophet to whom "the word of the Lord" came.

A few details about Joel can be supposed by reading his book. That the prophet lived in Jerusalem is probable because of his avid interest in the city. He makes repeated references to Zion, calls the people to assemble for worship, and shows much interest in the temple rituals and sacrifices.

This small prophetic book had much influence on the Day of Pentecost when the promised Spirit of God came upon Jesus' followers, not many days after His ascension. The apostle Peter proclaimed at that time that the new day of Spirit-filled people had arrived, just as it had been announced earlier by the prophet Joel (Acts 2:16–21).

DATE OF WRITING

The date of Joel's writing is unknown. It took place when the priests were in a position of strong authority; the Temple was standing; sacrifices were considered important; and certain foreign nations stood condemned. A more exact date, however, is impossible to determine. No mention is made of world empires, such as Assyria or Babylonia. No reference is made to Israel as the Northern Kingdom. No king is mentioned by name.

One suggested date for Joel's writing is early, before the Exile, around the time of the boy-king Joash (835–796 B.C.). Such an early date is considered partly because of the position of the book among the early prophets (Hosea, Amos) in the Hebrew canon. Further, the omission of a king's name would be appropriate if a young boy not yet mature, like Joash, sat on the throne.

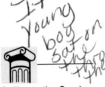

If a young boy sat on the throne

Selling to the Greeks

Joel's charge that the nations sold Judeans "to the Greeks" (Joel 3:6) does not help set a definite date for Joel's writing. Some time after 800 B.C., city-states began to develop in Greece. The high-water mark for the city-states was 500 to 404 B.C., during which period the dominant city-states were Athens and Sparta. Judeans could have been sold to Greeks any time from the eighth to the fourth centuries B.C.

Several arguments would favor a later date. After the Exile, there would be no need for announcing the coming destruction of Assyria or Babylon. No longer was there a king to mention or idolatrous high places to condemn. What Joel does mention fits the time of the returning exiles: worship centered in the Temple, the Grecian slave traffic (3:4–6), the scattering of Israelites and Judeans (3:2–6), and use of the term *Israel* to refer to Judah (2:27; 3:2).

AUDIENCE

To what community did Joel prophesy? The lack of historical information in the book makes this determination difficult. The only mention of "Israel" (2:27; 3:2) points not to the Northern Kingdom, but to all of God's people as His inheritance. Joel's interest in Mount Zion and Jerusalem (2:32; 3:1, 6, 20) suggests a Judean audience. Still, we know little of the situation facing Joel's listeners, among whom are listed drinkers of wine, farmers, priests, and elders. These were the groups that Joel called on to respond to the locust crisis in lamentation and repentance.

PURPOSE

The circumstance that provoked Joel's prophecy was a locust plague; the prophet's purpose was to warn Judah of the coming crisis. Further, he used the locust plague as a symbol for what God's judgment would be like. The invasion of the locusts was a point of reference to speak to the people of his own day about the coming day of the Lord. It would be a day on which God would exercise His judgments with awesome power. God would pour out His Spirit, judging all nations and blessing His people in a great day of salvation.

STRUCTURE AND CONTENT

The book of Joel has two natural divisions: the first section (1:1–2:17) covering the natural catastrophe of the locust plague and the second section (2:18–3:21) offering a message of salvation to God's repentant people. Both of these two sections are associated with the day of the Lord. Joel can warn of a present day of the Lord that will come with the locust plague, bringing judgment upon Judah (1:15; 2:1, 11). He can also promise a future day of the Lord that will witness a cosmic battle against the nations, bringing restoration of Judah's fortunes (2:31).

LITERARY STYLE

Joel uses a variety of literary forms, some associated with prophetic writings and others with priestly liturgy. Priestly forms are evident in the

Joel's Pentecost Prophecy

"These men are not drunk, as you suppose. It's only nine in the morning! No, this is what was spoken by the prophet Joel: 'In the last days, God says, I will pour out my Spirit on all people. Your sons and daughters will prophesy, your young men will see visions, your old men will dream dreams'" (Acts 2:15–17).

Some early theologians viewed the entire book of Joel as an allegory with the locusts representing four heathen nations that opposed God's people. Few scholars interpret Joel in this way today, but some believe that the oracle of the insect army (2:3–11) symbolizes a particular human army. Most likely, Joel intended the opposite: the images of a human army symbolize the destructive force of a locust swarm.

prayers of lamentation, appealing to God for help. A community lament calls on the people to pray (1:5–14), then the prophet adds his own personal lament (1:15–20). A summons for repentance (2:12–17) mixes a prophetic call to repent with a priestly ritual of response.

A common form of the writing prophets is the prophetic oracle. In Joel, a judgment oracle describes the locust invasion, using poetic imagery of a human army (2:1–11). A salvation oracle (2:18–27) provides the Lord's answer to the people's lament. Two oracles focus on God's activity in the end times: a short oracle of salvation (2:28–32) and a divine warrior hymn celebrating the defeat of Judah's enemies (3:1–21).

THEOLOGY

What are normally considered the great theological themes of Scripture are not to be found in Joel. He does not expound the deep love of God, as Hosea does. He does not cry out for social justice, as Amos does. He does not wrestle with the Assyrian and Babylonian destructions, as Isaiah and Jeremiah do. Joel treats one major theme—the day of the Lord.

In Joel we find two differing perspectives on the day of the Lord. One perspective deals with present catastrophe and judgment. The Creator God of all the universe can use calamities to bring His people to repentance, but afterwards, in pity, He will satisfy them with abundance. The second perspective deals with future promise and restoration. The same God can defeat all hostile powers to bring about a complete salvation for Judah. With both perspectives, Joel points to God as the only source of help.

THE MEANING OF JOEL FOR TODAY

A crisis involving swarms of locusts may seem far removed from us today. But whether we face locusts or some other emergency or dilemma, we must remember that God uses crises to sensitize His people to their utter dependence on God. Through the modern "plagues" that threaten us, God helps us realize our need for spiritual renewal.

Joel never details the nature of the people's sin. The details are unnecessary, for what was true of sin in Joel's day is true of our sin. Sin is serious and merits God's judgment. As Joel proclaimed then, judgment can be avoided by our heartfelt prayer and repentance. A gracious and merciful God desires to forgive His people and pour out His Spirit on them.

JOEL 1

A CALL FOR GOD'S PEOPLE TO RESPOND (1:1–2:17)

The first section of the book of Joel (1:1–2:17) describes a terrible plague of locusts that signals God's devastating action against the land. It concludes with a plea for confession of sins (2:12–17).

Witness to Future Generations (1:1–4)

Joel's use of the popular formula "The word of the LORD" demonstrates his devotion as God's prophet. As a prophet he distinguished himself from the other groups to which he wrote: elders (1:2), drunkards (1:5), farmers (1:11), and priests (1:13).

With the call "Hear this," Joel summoned the elders, along with all inhabitants of the land. As

Locusts

In the Middle East the locust periodically multiplies to astronomical numbers. As the swarm moves across the land, it devours all vegetation. Joel used different words—locust swarm, great locusts, young locusts, other locusts—which perhaps describe the insect at its various stages of life, from egg to larvae to adult insect (Joel 1:4).

leaders of the clans and tribes, the elders naturally assumed important roles in governing the affairs of the nation. The event that Joel announced would be of such significance that the ruling elders must be informed.

An unprecedented locust plague was symbolic of impending judgment. None of Judah's ancestors had witnessed anything of this magnitude in the past, and they are admonished to alert their children and grandchildren. By describing the plague in detail as involving a locust swarm, great locusts, young locusts, and other locusts, Joel possibly indicated four stages of the insects' development, moving through the land in successive swarms, destroying everything in their path. At the least he warns that Judah will be overwhelmed.

Mourn and Grieve over the Destruction (1:5–14)

Different groups within the community were called to lament the plague: drunkards, farmers, priests. Those who drank wine should weep, for locusts as powerful as a mighty nation would destroy the grapevines. No grape juice would be left to ferment.

The devastation of the land would be so great that farmers would be denied a harvest (1:11–12). Drought and famine followed the locust infiltration. Vegetation was stripped; the weather was hot; water was scarce.

Priests would mourn the loss of grain and wine. Without new wine, drink offerings would cease. Two of the main components for mixing grain offerings—fine flour and oil—would be unavailable. One of the primary functions of the priests, ministering with these offerings at the Temple, would be disrupted.

When misfortune strikes, creating a crisis that overcomes all human efforts, God is the only source to which we can turn. Joel gave the first admonition for the people to seek the Lord in fasting and prayer (1:14).

■ *The harvest was normally a festive occasion*
■ *for gathering the crops, usually marked by*
■ *religious festival. A feast of joy and thanks-*
■ *giving celebrated the completion of the har-*
■ *vest season. The locust plague, however, took*
■ *away any reason to celebrate, and the peo-*
■ *ple's harvest joy "withered away" (1:12).*

The Prophet Calls on God (1:15–20)

To Joel, the locust devastation indicated the imminent coming of the day of the Lord. Whereas the people of Judah had considered the day of the Lord as a time of punishment upon their enemies, Joel described it as "a dreadful day" for Judah itself. Animals desperately roamed the wasteland groaning and perishing for lack of food. Drought was so severe it could only be pictured as a fire devouring the land.

The prophet had already summoned the community to seek help from the Lord (1:14). Now Joel himself beseeched God with a personal plea. All of God's creation, from fields to streams to animals, was suffering, and the only hope was to call on the Lord.

QUESTIONS TO GUIDE YOUR STUDY

1. Why is it important to share with the younger generation our views and perspectives on events and happenings?

The Almighty

One Hebrew name for God is *Shaddai,* meaning "the Almighty" (Joel 1:15). It was particularly by this name that God was known to Abraham and the patriarchs (Gen. 17:1), although God Almighty was to some extent replaced by the name which God revealed to Moses: Yahweh, translated "the Lord." Joel's use of "Almighty" (Joel 1:15) emphasizes the power and majesty of the deity who would bring destruction on that dreadful day.

How can children benefit from the insights of adults?

2. Should people who are faithful to the Lord have any anxieties about the coming of the day of the Lord?

3. How do we as a congregation of God's people express our grief to God? How do we individually show God our grief?

The Shophar

The most frequently named musical instrument in the Bible is the "shophar," the ram's horn (Joel 2:1). Since its chief function was the making of noise, the shophar announced the new moon festivals and the Sabbaths, warned of approaching danger, and signaled the death of nobility. The instrument found a prominent place in Israel's life through its use in national celebrations (1 Kings 1:34).

JOEL 2

Chapter 2 repeats Joel's announcement for the people to assemble in Zion, on God's holy hill. They were to sound an alarm because the approaching day of the Lord will be dreadful.

The Army of Locusts (2:1–11)

The command is given to "blow the trumpet." The Hebrew *shophar* was a ram's horn that was used as a signaling instrument. In times of peace, the blowing of the shophar called the people together for ceremonies and assemblies. Sounding the horn for war prepared the Israelites to fight their enemies. The horn's signal this time was urgent, and those hearing it were advised to "tremble."

The impending danger is this day of the Lord, and it is near. Judah conceived the day of the Lord as a time of salvation for God's people; Joel corrected their concept. The day would bring darkness, gloom, clouds, and blackness, for it would witness a movement of troops across the land that would leave a path of devastation.

The "large and mighty army" (2:2) would bring destruction never experienced before nor ever to be experienced again. Presumably, this invading army is the plague of locusts swarming through the land. Before the awesome, destructive force of this army, a land resembling the garden of Eden will become a desert wasteland.

Joel associated the crisis of locusts with the day of the Lord. The insect invasion marked the onset of that day. It brought darkness by blotting out light from the sun, moon, and stars (2:10). The Lord Himself led the army; it is His army. Faced with an approaching force from the Almighty, Joel asked, "Who can endure it?"

- *Joel made it clear through his imagery of the*
- *insect army that God controls the destiny of*
- *His people. They are responsible to live in*
- *accordance with their covenantal relation-*
- *ship with Him. They will not be exempt from*
- *His vengeance on the approaching day.*

Rend Your Heart and Return (2:12–17)

Despite the approaching crisis, repentance was still appropriate. If the people repented, their gracious, patient God might have pity on them.

The Lord called on the people to fast, weep, and mourn. With the use of such outward tokens of repentance, the danger of pretense arose, for ritual not accompanied by a genuine attitude of repentance was empty. Nevertheless, the rituals themselves are not condemned. What was needed was not ritual alone, but the active involvement of people in making a radical change within the heart and in seeking a new direction for life.

The prophet did not specify the exact nature of Judah's sin, but he did describe the character of their God. Gracious, compassionate,

Military Imagery

By picturing the locust plague in military imagery (Joel 2:2–9), the prophet symbolized an overwhelming attack by a powerful human army. Similar imagery was used in other ancient Near Eastern literature. The images are human—cavalry, chariots, soldiers. Yet the actions are appropriate pictures of an insect army as it leaps, scales walls, runs along the wall, and climbs into houses.

Rending the Garments

Ancient people had certain practices associated with grief. One such practice was personal disfigurement. Sometimes they tore their garments; other times they wore sackcloth. These practices were probably done to convince onlookers that the person was really grieving. Mourners could convince the Lord by sincere emotions inwardly, in the heart, without tearing their clothes (Joel 2:13).

and abounding in love are the attributes that make it possible for God to relent of the coming calamity (2:13). Should He grant relief for the drought-stricken land, Judah will again be able to produce grain and drink offerings for worship.

Joel called the congregation, from the elderly to the nursing babies, to assemble for mourning (2:15–17). No one should excuse themselves, even for an event such as a wedding (2:16). The priests functioned as intermediaries, pleading to God on behalf of the people. They reminded God that a fallen Judah would be cause for other nations to mock God as a deity who cannot preserve His own people (2:17).

■ *Rending hearts instead of garments pictured*
■ *a sincere repentance. Joel attacked any form*
■ *of feigned worship, calling on each person to*
■ *show genuine contrition. While humans*
■ *place importance on outward appearance,*
■ *the Lord "looks at the heart" (1 Sam. 16:7).*

GOD RESPONDS TO HIS PEOPLE (2:18–3:21)

The second section of the book of Joel (2:18–3:21), written in the form of a first-person response from God, proclaims hope for the repentant people coupled with judgment upon their enemies. Previously, Joel's theme was judgment; now, it is salvation.

God Will Have Pity (2:18–27)

There was hope beyond judgment on that day. On the basis of Judah's repentance, God answered that He would show pity and remove the plague. The threat of swarming locusts was reversed, as the insect army was driven back—some into the desert, some into the Dead Sea, some into the Mediterranean. The land will again produce grain, new wine, and oil.

The fear and shame of the people is now replaced by joy and praise (2:21–24). Testimony rings out, confirming that God has delivered the land. Three groups—the land, the wild animals, the people—are instructed to rejoice over the "great things" which the Lord has done.

Once the people truly repented, God could restore the land, and the people would know God was present in Judah, protecting them. In its most basic sense, salvation is the saving of lives from death or harm, and so the Lord's salvation delivers Judah from the plague. Because God is the source of salvation, any action—even when the focus is on deliverance from locusts—is a saving act. Judah would know that He alone is God (2:27).

The Day of the Lord (2:28–32)

The prophet told of God's salvation from the locust plague (2:17–27). The locust plague was used to tell about a greater day of the Lord in the future. Joel anticipated a future time when God's people are promised the presence of God's Spirit among them. They will be filled with God's Spirit, and they will prophesy.

A great outpouring of the Spirit would bring a wonderful renewal. Mount Zion and Jerusalem would be the site of the deliverance, where all who call on the Lord would be saved.

This day would witness "wonders in the heavens" (2:30). The sun would not give its light, and the moon would be turned to blood (2:31). These cosmic signs attest to the power of God.

Locusts into the Sea

Joel prophesied of God driving the locusts into the eastern and western seas (Joel 2:20), recalling an earlier plague ended the same way. At the time of the Exodus, the eighth plague in Egypt consisted of locusts throughout the land. The plague ended when "the LORD changed the wind to a very strong west wind, which caught up the locusts and carried them into the Red Sea" (Exod. 10:19).

They Will Prophesy

Joel looked forward to a time when the Spirit of God would be upon all people, even male and female servants (Joel 2:28–29). All could become prophets, with no exclusions, no go-betweens, and all could know God's salvation. This prophetic hope was fulfilled at Pentecost (Acts 2:17–18) and in the ongoing life of the early church.

They witness God's presence on that terrible day and the climax and consummation of His purposes for the universe.

■ *The emphasis of the future day of the Lord is*
■ *on "everyone" (2:32). In that great time, sal-*
■ *vation will be available to all who seek God,*
■ *without distinction of age, gender, or social*
■ *status.*

QUESTIONS TO GUIDE YOUR STUDY

1. What are the differences between God's salvation from the locusts (2:18–27) and His salvation on the final day of the Lord (2:28–32)?

2. What are the relationships among judgment, repentance, mercy, and salvation?

3. The people were instructed to return to God "even now" (2:12). Why should we not delay in our decision to repent and turn to God in faith?

JOEL 3

Chapter 3 pictures a phase of the great day of the Lord when the nations are gathered for judgment. The event is some time in the future, described as "in those days and at that time" (3:1). The Lord will triumph over His enemies so completely on that day that foreigners will never again invade Judah.

God Will Judge All Nations (3:1–8)

One aspect of the future day of the Lord is the restoration of Judah; the other aspect is judgment upon the nations. Eventually all nations will be judged by God in the Valley of Jehoshaphat (3:2). The name "Jehoshaphat," meaning "the Lord judges," is probably symbolic of God's judging all nations at His place of judgment.

The nations are charged with committing violence against God's inheritance—His own people Israel (referring to the Northern and Southern Kingdoms). They have exiled the people and seized their land, while trading and selling them into slavery. The sentence against the nations will be the same fate, as they too would be sold as slaves to a distant country—the Sabeans (3:8).

Tyre, Sidon, and Philistia are called by name. They are charged with looting God's Temple and selling Judean slaves to the Greeks (3:4–6). These cities were great trading centers whose commerce in human slaves was hardly interrupted by the rise and fall of surrounding empires. Two other nations, Egypt and Edom, are mentioned later (3:19).

Valley of Jehoshaphat

No evidence exists that any valley actually bore the name "Jehoshaphat" in Joel's time (Joel 3:2). Since the fourth century A.D. the Kidron Valley has been known as the Valley of Jehoshaphat, though it is not certain Joel referred to the Kidron Valley. The prophet may have used the name to indicate the place to which the Lord would summon the nations for judgment.

- *The concept of God as judge rendering judgments focuses on His authority as Sovereign over His people Israel and over all peoples.*
- *Joel prophesied of a time when God would exercise His judgment with awesome power in the day of the Lord.*

War Against the Nations (3:9–17)

Following the charges, the nations are summoned to assemble in the Valley of Jehoshaphat, where God sits in judgment (3:12). They must prepare for a war they cannot win. God's role as judge, issuing righteous verdicts, is

Plowshares and Pruning Hooks

In Joel's agricultural imagery, farming instruments will be converted to weapons of war. This action reverses the similar prophecies of Isaiah and Micah: "They will beat their swords into plowshares and their spears into pruning hooks" (Isa. 2:4; Mic. 4:3). The day of the Lord will not be a time of peace for the wicked nations facing God's judgment.

emphasized by calling the assembly location the "valley of decision" (3:14).

Changes in the heavens (sun, moon, and stars are darkened) mark this event as the day of the Lord. Though earth and sky will tremble, the people of Israel will find a refuge and stronghold in the Lord. From these climactic happenings, Israel will know assuredly that the Lord their God dwells in their midst, in Zion, and will not allow His holy city to be invaded again (3:17).

God Will Bless His People (3:18–21)

Both aspects of the day of the Lord, judgment and restoration, are in view as Joel closed the book. For Judah, the day would bring unparalleled prosperity, but Egypt and Edom could look for terrible punishment. Representing all nations that have treated Judah violently, Egypt and Edom will become desolate, as was Judah during the locust plague (2:3). Judah, though, would experience a complete transformation. The land once desolate and dried up because of the plague would produce an abundance of new wine, milk, and water. All of these blessings are because "the LORD dwells in Zion" (3:21).

■ *The day of the Lord is a time in which God*
■ *displays His sovereign initiative to reveal His*
■ *control of history, time, His people, and all*
■ *people. Those who know themselves to be*
■ *God's people can trust God to be present with*
them and to deliver them.

QUESTIONS TO GUIDE YOUR STUDY

1. The nations used Judah's people for slaves. Have you ever been tempted to

treat a person as a "thing" in order to benefit yourself? How many different ways do we "use" people for our own advantage?

2. Why are people more interested in the timing of the "last days" than they are in living a life pleasing to God?

3. What attributes of God lead to His willingness to pardon? What condition must we meet in order to seek God's pardon?

THE BOOK OF OBADIAH

The book of Obadiah is the shortest book of the minor prophets, preserving the message of Obadiah, the prophet. While the name "Obadiah" is a common name in the Old Testament, no source outside of this book mentions the prophet Obadiah.

Obadiah's prophecy concerns approaching judgment on the nation of Edom, a small mountainous land east of the Dead Sea. The Edomites were considered descendants of Esau, and thus were related to the Judahites through descent from the patriarch Abraham. Despite this link of ancestry, Judah and Edom lived in tension with each other throughout Israel's period in Canaan. The book of Obadiah reflects this tension.

AUTHOR

The title of the book reveals nothing about the prophet except his name. The meaning of his name is "servant of Yahweh," possibly reflecting his parents' faith and spiritual ambitions for their child.

Speaking for God

Prophets often marked the beginning of their prophecy with the formula, "Thus says the LORD." Similarly, Obadiah begins his message with an expanded formula: "This is what the Sovereign LORD says" (Obad. 1:1). The formula reinforces Obadiah's call as a prophet, emphasizing that God is behind the message. Prophets were not all-knowing but all-telling—they told what God had told them to tell.

oBadiah means

The prophet's family and homeland are unknown. What is known is that Obadiah was a prophet of Yahweh. The title, "vision of Obadiah," turns attention to the book's divine author, since "vision" was a technical term for a prophetic revelation from God.

DATE OF WRITING

Prophetic books often give the names of kings who reigned when a particular prophet was active. Since the book of Obadiah mentions no king, the book may have been written after Judah's monarchy had ended.

The book dates from a time when Judah and Jerusalem were in ruins and when relations with Edom were hostile. Historically, this situation fits with the early postexilic period, at the end of the sixth century B.C. Obadiah's list of Edom's crimes (Obad. 1:11–14) reflects the fall of Jerusalem to the Babylonians in 586 B.C., concentrating on the part the Edomites played in that tragic event. Furthermore, the Edomites filled the vacuum caused by Judah's exile by moving west and annexing the Negev to the south of Judah. Obadiah looks forward to Jerusalem's exiles regaining that land (Obad. 1:20).

The fall of Edom occurred around 500 B.C. So the most probable date for Obadiah to have recorded his vision would be some time between 586 and 500 B.C.

AUDIENCE

Although the entire book of Obadiah deals with God's approaching judgment on Edom, the audience for Obadiah's words probably did not consist of Edomites. No evidence suggests that Obadiah traveled to Edom to deliver a message of judgment to the Edomites themselves. The writings of the prophets against foreign nations were usually written for the benefit of God's people. Obadiah probably addressed his message to Judahites.

Judah reacted to Edom's aggressions with a strong sense of grievance. Obadiah's oracle responds to an underlying impassioned prayer of lament, in which Judah appealed to God to act as a providential trial judge to set the situation right.

PURPOSE

The aim of Obadiah is to sustain faith in God's moral government and hope in the eventual triumph of His just will. It brings the message that God is on the throne and cares for His own.

The justice of God is evident in two emphases of Obadiah's message. First, Judah's enemies would be punished. Edom would receive just recompense for her aggressions against Judah. Second, Judah would receive comfort and hope through the promise of restoration to their land.

Yet, Obadiah's purpose ranges far beyond the relationship of Judah and Edom. Edom, in a sense, represents all nations of the world who oppose God's people. All nations will receive just recompense for their deeds. Furthermore, Judah's and Israel's reoccupation of the land will be permanent, for, from this time on, "the kingdom will be the LORD's" (Obad. 1:21).

STRUCTURE AND CONTENT

Though a short book, Obadiah divides its message into four oracles. Oracle 1 (Obad. 1:1c–4) exposes Edom's root problem—pride. The oracle carries the authority of God, as indicated by the oracle formula, "declares the LORD," which ends the section. Oracle 2 (Obad. 1:5–10) describes the extent to which Edom will be

Edom

Edom was an area southeast and southwest of the Dead Sea, on opposite sides of the Arabah. The Edomite area was largely wilderness—semi-desert, not very conducive to agriculture—and many of the inhabitants were semi-nomads. Thus, the boundaries of Edom would have been rather ill-defined, a situation that caused tension with neighbors such as Judah. The center of Edomite population was the capital of Bozrah.

destroyed. Oracle 3 (Obad. 1:11–14) details the unbrotherly conduct with which Edom had mistreated Judah. God's judgment and justice come into view in oracle 4 (Obad. 1:15–21), which focuses on the day of the Lord.

LITERARY STYLE

As is typical of the Old Testament prophetic books, Obadiah is almost all poetry. Only the title (Obad. 1:1a, b) appears in prose format. In the Hebrew language, poetry provides imagery and tone for inspired writers to drive God's word home to His people.

THEOLOGY

God is just and holds responsible those who take advantage of others in their time of distress. The Edomites forgot that they and the Judahites shared a common ancestor—Abraham the patriarch. By mistreating Judah, Edom fell victim to God's promise to Abraham: "I will bless those who bless you, and whoever curses you I will curse" (Gen. 12:3). After the Babylonian invasion, the Edomites should have brought blessing to their brother Judahites, but they did not.

More significant than Edom's deserved punishment and even than Judah's restoration is Obadiah's final note. The day of the Lord will result in the universal rule of God. The Lord will reign over all nations and all peoples; truly "the kingdom will be the LORD's" (Obad. 1:21). Facing a great distress, the writer of the book of Revelation found comfort in words that echo Obadiah's: "The kingdom of the world has become the kingdom of our Lord and of his Christ" (Rev. 11:15).

Pride of Your Heart

Edom's basic problem is summarized by the phrase, "pride of your heart" (Obad. 1:3). Pride is easier to recognize in others than in ourselves. It is the opposite of humility, the proper attitude to have in relation to God. A proud attitude toward God affects a person's attitude toward others, often causing a proud person to have a low estimate of the worth of others and therefore to treat others with contempt. Beware of pride in your heart, which is the root of sin.

THE MEANING OF OBADIAH FOR TODAY

The Babylonian invasion of Jerusalem and Edom's capture of Judahite fugitives are events that seem far removed from our day-to-day experiences. Misfortune, though, comes in a myriad of forms and is common to human experience across the ages. Also common is the activity of those who take advantage of our misfortunes and rejoice in the gains they make at our expense.

The book of Obadiah speaks to us in such situations. Obadiah addresses the manner in which we might respond to those who mistreat us. Obadiah examines the degree to which we either trust God to be just or take matters into our own hands.

OBADIAH

Obadiah and Jeremiah

THE PRIDE OF EDOM (VV. 1–4)

The first oracle of Obadiah (Obad. 1:1–4) pertains to Edom's pride. Pride deceives people into thinking they can escape God's judgment. Edom would discover that such an escape was impossible.

Obadiah 1:1c–4 duplicates a similar passage in Jeremiah 49:14–16. Some differences between the passages do exist, so either Jeremiah or Obadiah borrowed from the other, or both prophets borrowed from an earlier source.

The Title of the Book (vv. 1a, b)

The title verse of Obadiah calls this book "a vision." In fact, the entire book is a vision picturing God's decisions about Edom.

"I have heard a message from the LORD: An envoy was sent to the nations to say, 'Assemble yourselves to attack it! Rise up for battle!' Now I will make you small among the nations, despised among men. The terror you inspire and the pride of your heart have deceived you, you who live in the clefts of the rocks, who occupy the heights of the hill. Though you build your nest as high as the eagle's, from there I will bring you down,' declares the LORD" (Jer. 49:14–16).

Among the classical prophets, including Amos, Hosea, Isaiah, and Micah, the vision was the primary means of communication between God and the prophet. "Vision" and "Word of Yahweh" became synonymous in these prophetic writings. So the "vision of Obadiah" could refer to the manner in which the prophet Obadiah received a message from Yahweh concerning Edom.

The book of Obadiah, however, is not an account of a prophetic vision concerning Edom. It does not reveal Obadiah's prophetic experience in which he received God's message. Rather, it is a report of "what the Sovereign LORD says about Edom" (Obad. 1b). The book presents the content of God's message to Obadiah—the knowledge that God revealed to His prophet.

Through the avenue of visions, the prophets interpreted the meaning of immediate events in the history of Israel. The role that Edom played in Judah's fall in 586 B.C. was apparently long remembered by Judahites and significant enough to be the subject of Obadiah's vision.

Pride Goes Before a Fall (vv. 1c–4)

Obadiah graphically portrayed God's judgment on Edom when it would be humbled and eventually destroyed.

An envoy calls for battle (v. 1c). Obadiah speaks of the message "we have heard." By "we," the prophet possibly referred to himself and other prophets who heard God's message. Or else he used "we" to mean himself and the people of God to whom he prophesied. He emphasized his source: God had given him the message; it was "from the LORD."

Already God was inviting the nations to assemble for a battle against Edom. Already a coalition of neighboring groups was planning to attack Edom. They would serve as the Lord's instrument to execute His judgment.

Edom will be brought down (vv. 2–4). Addressing Edom, God promised to defeat these people who considered themselves invincible. Their lofty self-conceit is reflected in the descriptions of Edom's fortress city, Sela. They imagined themselves to be safe, for they dwelt "on the heights" with their major city built "in the clefts of the rocks."

Pride and self-conceit usually surface in great boasting. This was certainly true for the Edomites, who boasted that no one could bring them "down to the ground." Such haughty self-sufficiency fails to consider divine power. God would topple Edom's mountain community.

"Rock" City

The Edomites are described as those "who live in the clefts of the rocks" (Obad. 1:3). The Hebrew word *Sela* is a noun referring to rocky country. But "Sela" is also the place name of a major fortified city in Edom, which Judah had once captured (2 Kings 14:7). So the Edomites lived in the clefts of Sela, the rocky city.

■ *The Edomites based their sense of security on*
■ *their rock fortress, believing it to be invinci-*
■ *ble. When we trust in our own strength,*
■ *wealth, or power rather than in God, we set*
■ *ourselves up to be humbled. Like Edom, we*
■ *too will be made small. Hopefully, being*
■ *brought down will cause us to "look up" to*
■ *the Sovereign Lord.*

"I Will Bring You Down"

"Pride goes before destruction, a haughty spirit before a fall" (Prov. 16:18).

THE CERTAIN DEFEAT OF EDOM (VV. 5–10)

The second oracle of Obadiah (Obad. 1:5–10) spells ultimate defeat for Edom. Their allies would let them down, and neither their famed wisdom nor their warriors would be able to save them.

Announcing Complete Destruction (vv. 5–7)

Two illustrations from life's experiences warn of total destruction for Edom. When thieves rob a house and when grape pickers harvest a field, they leave something behind. Thieves take what they consider valuable, leaving the rest; grape pickers leave the gleanings. Edom, however, will be picked clean!

Edom Falls

The end of Edom as an independent nation possibly came at the hands of Nabonidus, the last king of the Neo-Babylonian Empire (555–539 B.C.). After 552 B.C. Nabonidus campaigned in southern Transjordan and northern Arabia, destroying cities along the way. Other peoples would control Edom's land. By New Testament times a people of Arabic origin known as the Nabateans had established a commercial empire with its center in the formerly Edomite territory east of the Arabah. The whole region southeast of the Dead Sea came to be known as Nabatea.

The Edomites, as descendants of Esau, Jacob's brother (Gen. 25:24–26), were closely related to the Israelites and Judahites. Thus, Edom occasionally is called Israel's "brother" (Amos 1:11). Edom, brother Esau, would be pillaged.

Deceitful people can become the targets of deceit themselves. We should not be surprised that people who deceive would have difficulty building loyalty among their various relationships and associations. Edom's downfall would be instigated by those who once had been allies and friends.

Human Wisdom and Strength Fail (vv. 8–9)

If reliance on allies would fail Edom, so also would reliance on self. The loss of Edom's wise men meant the loss of understanding needed to deal with its situation. The loss of warriors would leave the Edomites defenseless.

Your Brother Jacob (v. 10)

Conspiracy against a "brother" cannot remain unpunished. The mention of violence against Jacob in verse 10 points to the reason for Edom's doom. The verse forms a transition from the judgment of God described in Obadiah 1:5–9 to the detailed picture of Edom's cold-hearted betrayal of Judah in Obadiah 1:11–14. That betrayal would result in a severe, humiliating, and shameful penalty.

- *Edomites had relied on their wise men for*
- *understanding. But committing violent deeds*
- *against Judah, the people of God, was utter*
- *foolishness. Worldly wisdom often seems*
- *desirable to us, but spiritually may make no*
- *sense at all. We must learn that the fear of*
- *the Lord is true wisdom.*

EDOM'S ABUSE OF JUDAH (VV. 11–14)

The third oracle of Obadiah (Obad. 1:11–14) lists the various actions that comprised Edom's unbrotherly conduct toward Judah. The catalog of crimes functions as the accusation which warranted God's verdict of punishment upon Edom.

Standing Aloof (v. 11)

The first crime was not something Edom did, but rather something it did not do. When Jerusalem was falling to the Babylonians in 586 B.C., the Edomites, along with others, failed to come to Judah's aid. Because Edom "stood aloof" while foreigners looted Jerusalem, it acted like a foreigner.

Rejoicing and Boasting (v. 12)

A second crime was Edom's attitude toward Judah and Judah's predicament. The Edomites looked down on Judah with an attitude of superiority, even boasting. Judah's misfortune should have roused sorrow and compassion from the Edomites, who rejoiced instead.

Seizing the Wealth (v. 13)

Remaining on the sidelines with a self-righteous, malicious attitude was wrong. Yet the Edomites played an even more active role in Jerusalem's

Sins of Omission

One charge against Edom was that, during Judah's distress, they simply "stood aloof" (Obad. 1:11). Despite treaty ties with Judah, the Edomites, along with others, failed to come to Judah's aid. Sometimes a position of noninvolvement, when we know we should get involved, is wrong. As James says, "Anyone, then, who knows the good he ought to do and doesn't do it, sins" (Jas. 4:17).

Jerusalem Falls

Judah's King Zedekiah revolted against Babylon in 588 B.C., a move which led to the ultimate fall of Jerusalem in 586 B.C. Bablyon's King Nebuchadnezzar razed the Jerusalem Temple as his army moved into the city. Edom even helped the Babylonian invaders by looting Jerusalem and handing over Judahite refugees (Obad. 1:13–14).

tragic event. They actually helped Babylon by participating in the looting of Jerusalem.

Handing Over Refugees (v. 14)

To seize a person's wealth is to violate that person's right of ownership. Yet Edom committed a far worse evil. As Judahites fled the invading Babylonians, the Edomites captured the fugitives, handing them over to the Babylonian army.

- ■ *The behavior of the Edomites ran the gamut*
- ■ *from failing to do what was right to display-*
- ■ *ing an evil spirit and actively participating*
- ■ *in the wrongful destruction of the Judahites'*
- ■ *lives. How do we compare when we examine*
- ■ *our "brotherly" and "sisterly" treatment of*
- ■ *others? We must not rationalize selfish con-*
- ■ *duct, assuming it to be justified because of*
- ■ *"circumstances."*

THE DAY OF THE LORD (vv. 15–21)

The fourth and last oracle of Obadiah (Obad. 1:15–21) focuses on the day of the Lord. In Old Testament theology the concept of the day of the Lord embraces not only God's people but their neighbors as well. Obadiah prophesied the full scope of this coming day. It would bring judgment for the nations (Obad. 1:15–16), but deliverance for God's people (Obad. 1:17–21).

Edom's Judgment (vv. 15–16)

When the Old Testament prophets spoke and wrote of the "day of the LORD," they were using a term familiar to their audience. The people expected the day of the Lord to bring light and salvation, but prophets warned that for some people the day would bring darkness and judgment (see Amos 5:18).

Edom's destruction would be part of the day of the Lord. Indeed, the fall of Edom would trigger an eschatological event in which order would be restored to an unruly world. This wider dimension is reflected in verses 15–16. The judgments that would fall on Edom were not isolated events, but one facet of a judgment that would affect "all nations."

The urgency of Obadiah's message is that the day "is near" (v. 15). For Edom, this was not good news because on this day sinful Edom would receive a just recompense: as Edom had done to Judah, so it would be done to Edom.

Edom reveled in the Babylonian victory over Judah, even drinking on Mount Zion—God's holy hill (v. 16). On the day of the Lord, Edom and all the nations will be continually drinking, but not in revelry. Instead, they will drink from the cup of God's judgment and wrath.

Drinking the Cup

In the Bible, images of cups and drinking are used in a figurative sense for God's wrath (Obad. 1:16). The contents of the cup are sometimes accentuated, since symbolically God serves the drink of punishment. Drinking of the cup portrays the totality of divine judgment on the wicked—"the LORD, the God of Israel, said to me: 'Take from my hand this cup filled with the wine of my wrath and make all the nations to whom I send you drink it'" (Jer. 25:15).

- *What began as a feud between the brothers*
- *Esau and Jacob escalated over the years to an*
- *ongoing conflict between two nations: Edom*
- *and Judah. We must watch for bitterness*
- *within ourselves and erase it through for-*
- *giveness, lest a small disagreement result in*
- *a major war.*

Judah's Deliverance (vv. 17–18)

The day of the Lord would bring destruction for Edom, but deliverance for Zion and Israel. God's people would be vindicated not for their own sakes but as earthly witnesses to God's glory.

The coming day of the Lord will witness a reversal of fortunes. Both Israel and Judah had turned from God and were punished in exile. When Judah fell, Edom mistreated the Judahite survivors (Obad. 1:14). Now the tables would be turned. A reunited Judah and Israel, represented as the "house of Jacob" and "house of Joseph," would serve as the instruments of God's judgment—fire and flame—and destroy the house of Esau (the Edomites) as though they were stubble.

Restoring the Land (vv. 18–21)

Obadiah presents the most complete plan for the resettlement of the Israelite tribes in Canaan to be found in any of the prophets. The remnant of God's people would reoccupy the land from various directions. From the Negev, from the foothills, and from the fields they would come to regain the old territory they previously occupied and to expand into new territory.

The days following Jerusalem's fall to the Babylonians can be considered Judah's worst of times. Yet during these dark days, the vision of Obadiah ends with a stirring call to faith: "the kingdom will be the LORD's" (Obad. 1:21). In this new kingdom, God's enemies are destroyed, God's people govern in the restored land, and God's rule is established over all nations of the world.

Esau and Jacob

From the first, tension characterized the relationship of the brothers Esau and Jacob. Esau, the extrovert, was a favorite of his father and as a hunter provided him with his favorite meats. Jacob was the favorite of his mother Rebekah. Animosity between the descendants of the two brothers continued across the centuries, being reflected in Obadiah's prophecy of struggle between the house of Jacob and the house of Esau (Obad. 1:18).

- When the injustices of this lifetime become
- difficult for us to understand, we must place
- our trust in God's ultimate justice. Rather
- than focusing on specific conflicts which we
- have experienced, let us keep in view the final
- outcome that God has planned for history.

QUESTIONS TO GUIDE YOUR STUDY

1. Why does a humble person often possess a more realistic perception of his or her self-worth than does the proud person?

2. Can you think of a situation in which you wronged someone because you failed to act on his or her behalf? In what ways was your inactivity harmful to that person's welfare?

3. Have you ever found yourself "feeling glad" over the misfortune of another person? What factors made it seem "right" to find joy in someone else's pain?

The following list is a collection of source works that will provide either more specific information on the books of Hosea, Joel, Amos, and Obadiah or an expanded treatment of themes and topics related to these books.

Birch, Bruce C., *Hosea, Joel, and Amos* (Westminster Bible Companion). A lay-level volume that explains the original historical context and probes for the modern-day significance of each Bible book.

Holman Bible Dictionary. An exhaustive, alphabetically arranged resource of Bible-related subjects. An excellent tool of definitions and other information on the people, places, things, and events of the Bible.

Holman Bible Handbook. A comprehensive treatment of Hosea, Joel, Amos, and Obadiah that offers outlines, commentary on key themes and sections, and full-color photos, illustrations, charts, and maps. Provides an emphasis on the broader theological message of each book.

NIV Disciple's Study Bible. A study Bible offering over ten thousand annotations on the Bible. A valuable resource for relating the message of the minor prophets to the key doctrines of the Christian faith. Provides a theological introduction to each book of the Bible, as well as insights for putting faith into practice.

Smith, Billy K., and Frank S. Page, *Amos, Obadiah, Jonah* (The New American Commentary), vol. 19b. A more scholarly treatment of the text of the prophets that provides emphases on the text itself, background, and theological considerations.

Smith, Billy K., *Hosea, Joel, Amos, Obadiah, Jonah* (Layman's Bible Book Commentary). A popular-level treatment of these prophetical books. This easy-to-use volume provides a relevant and practical perspective.